YOU AND ME MAKE THREE

Also by Phil Murray

YOU CAN ALWAYS GET WHAT YOU WANT
BEFORE THE BEGINNING IN THOUGHT
EMPOWERMENT
THE 49 STEPS TO A BRIGHT LIFE
BITES ON PERSONAL DEVELOPMENT
STAYING AWAKE FOREVER
THE FLOW OF LIFE

YOU AND ME MAKE THREE

Understanding this extraordinary
equation will change your life

Phil Murray

Hodder & Stoughton

Copyright © 1998 by Phil Murray
Illustrations by Soozi

First published in Great Britain in 1998 by Perfect Words and Music
Published in 2000 by Hodder and Stoughton
A division of Hodder Headline PLC

The right of Phil Murray to be identified as the Author of the Work
has been asserted by him in accordance with the Copyright,
Designs and Patents Act 1988.

10 9 8 7 6 5 4 3 2 1

All rights reserved. No part of this publication may be reproduced, stored
in a retrieval system, or transmitted, in any form or by any means without
the prior written permission of the publisher, nor be otherwise circulated
in any form of binding or cover other than that in which it is published
and without a similar condition being imposed on the subsequent purchaser.

A CIP catalogue record for this title is available
from the British Library.

ISBN 0 340 71794 7

Printed and bound in Great Britain by
Mackays of Chatham PLC, Chatham, Kent

Hodder and Stoughton
A division of Hodder Headline PLC
338 Euston Road
London NW1 3BH

This book is dedicated
to making the difference

CONTENTS

WHAT IS THIS ALL ABOUT? *an introduction*	9
INNOMINATE *in the beginning*	13
INNOMINATE WENT TO MARKET	19
AN ATOM A HUMAN AND THE PLANET A Little About Radiation	25
INNO VISITS DEATH	35
INNOMINATE GIRDS ITS LOINS	40
INNO ENCOUNTERS TECHNOLOGY	43
INNO'S MISSION	50
DON'T CHANGE NUTTIN For The First Little While	55
INNOMINATE AND THE MANDALA	60
WHAT IS PERSONAL PSYCHOLOGY?	66
INNOMINATE ENCOUNTERS SANAT KUMARA	76
HOW TO CREATE A SOLAR SYSTEM	85
INNO AND THE ANGELS	91
CAUSES OF DECISION TO IMPROVE PERSONAL LIFE	97
INNOMINATE TACKLES THE CYNICS	102

THE ODESSA PHIAL Sasha Flies To London	108
INNO'S PHYSICAL CHALLENGE	116
MANUAL	123
INNOMINATE WAGES A HOLY WAR Battleground Earth	129
INNER POWER	136
INNOMINATE MEETS THE BANK MANAGER	142
WHAT HAPPENS WHEN YOU MAKE A WISH	149
INNO AND THE GRAIN OF PARADISE	155
THOUGHT CONTROL	160
INNOMINATE'S MAGIC THREES	166
FAMILIES And How To Thrive In Them	172
INNOMINATE STANDS FOR PARLIAMENT	180
STOCK LETTER FROM A SILENT KNIGHT	187
TELLING THE TRUTH HONESTLY	195
THE TRUTH BEHIND ALL RELIGIONS	202
INNOMINATE TELLS A LIE	208
WHEN TO BEGIN THE MAGICAL EQUATION?	211
THE END	218

As the old sea captain walked the beach at dawn, he noticed a young girl in the distance picking up starfish and flinging them into the sea. Finally catching up with her, the retired sailor asked why she was doing this. The answer was that the stranded starfish would die if left until the morning sun appeared ...

"But the beach goes on for miles and there are millions of stranded starfish," stated the captain, "how can your efforts make any difference?"

The young girl looked at the starfish in her hand before throwing it to safety in the waves ...

"It makes a difference to that one," she answered.

WHAT IS THIS ALL ABOUT?
an introduction ...

It is not often that something so simple as 1+1=3 comes along to change your life. Of course, the equation itself is powerless, so this book sets out to explore the human increase in potential which can occur when the idea of interdependence, being the backbone of this formula, is allowed to freely intermingle with all aspects of life.

To illustrate this potential however, I have not set out in linear fashion to explain all from a scientific and logical viewpoint; rather, I have seized the opportunity to treat holistically, a concept, on which in fact, the whole of our knowable universe is based. This entails discussion of as wide a diversity of topics as can be aesthetically included in a work of this size.

Now the temptation for any author given free reign as I have, to undertake such exploration, is to lean into mystical realms, and prey on the fascinating yet not always pragmatic tendencies for humans to become fixated on the invisible side of life, by writing a treatise which is stimulating to read, but useless to implement. I have not, but if it appears so, then it is in your interpretation of my words that will germinate such failing.

Each chapter is designed to be read and then pondered. The overall idea is that each section contains within it the embryonic form of a personal cognition for you. A successful dawning of new horizons into your consciousness hovers throughout the pages, and within each idea lurks a self realisation, for you, waiting to happen. If it does not work in this fashion, and this may well be the case for you and me, but if we do not make three, it will be you and not me who has not pondered the postulates, potentials and truisms contained herein.

This is not a transposed lecture or words adapted from another medium. It is a book written especially for the growing numbers of human beings who now sense with greater clarity as each day passes, that there is indeed more to life than meets the eye. When this happens, it is not always with like minded people that you will find yourself. You may wish to discuss certain happenings which will cross your consciousness from time to time, and for this reason, I run THE POSITIVE ATTITUDE CLUB, which is a kind of *non profit making after sales service,* to describe it in commercial terms, but really, it is a concept which you may carry with you at all times. The PAC, as it is more widely acronymically known, is also a creative discussion forum which meets regularly within my immediate physical sphere of operation, and more widely when others who have cognited on the usefulness of the concept, get down to the business of organising meetings themselves. For those not averse to a modicum of bureaucracy, a form appears at the end of this book through which you can make contact with me. Of course a straightforward letter will also do that trick, and I am pledged to address all of my correspondence personally.

So, sit back, relax, and let your mind wander wherever it will take you; from time to time you will be asked to exert will over your inner world of total human potential, and at other times you may wonder why on earth you are reading descriptions of seemingly unrelated events more relevant to my life than yours. How you handle any awkward vicissitudes of this nature is again for you to ponder; at no time will my ideas ever take precedent over your own. I will not ever ask that you adopt my viewpoints and discard your own, without thought and good reason.

If you find yourself much the same after finishing this book then it will not have worked for you. It is in *the practice* of any self realisations that your true growth through association with myself and this book will be apparent. You and me make three, but only if we get down to the business of making it so!

    In this you have my total commitment forever … with love …

Phil Murray

INNOMINATE
in the beginning

A woman and a man had a baby; no matter what they did or how this couple thought, they found that it was impossible to wholly mould their new offspring into the image of its forebears. There were signs which saw optimism rise to the effervescent smiles of the hopeful parents, including appearance, certain tastes and the occasional preference, but such hints were mere transient symptoms of a socialisation process almost impossible to eradicate without dedication to utter creative freedom.

Frightened by what they saw in their child as rebellion, refusal to conform and general devilry, they wondered, quite against all that had been inculcated into them through generations of repeated and uncorrected aphorisms, what would happen if they allowed their adored protégé total freedom of all that a being can be free from ... but it was too late for such an absolute to be possible, if indeed it could have happened had they decided on such a course of action earlier.

When the child was ready to leave its parents and begin the process of procreation all over again with a mate of its own, the parents realised something so simple, yet of a profundity which if assimilated into the workings of humanity, would become the fundamental of a useful initiation for billions of incarnate souls at once, and herald the dawning of a new horizon so vast and powerful as to render all human thought up to that date on par with our viewpoint of the mind mechanisms currently existent in the lives of orang-utans!

The dependent possessed something, which, if it were possible to reduce that child to its constituent parts formed from the mother and father in this case, would be left behind as a manifestation seemingly without physical parentage. We can call it a soul if title is required, but there is more to this mystery than conventional spiritual explanations have hitherto explained, and it is this ... when two things, spirits, souls, lives, minds, stones, plants or animals, join together with creative aspiration, a third force is always created which cannot be simplified into its integral components.

Some may call this a kind of alchemy which it is, or perhaps more accurately it is simple chemistry, but an aspect of this science up until now unexplored by any but the most adventurous and esoteric ...

1+1=3

We have the opportunity as had the parents already mentioned, to end all reverence to silly socialisation processes which see us inculcating, into children ever more ready for new horizons, habits which are no further along the evolutionary line than is the continuance of an anthropomorphic god sitting in judgement on a heavenly throne as figurehead to all of our spiritual aspirations.

The equation is not new; only our recognition of it is fresh. Not many people have time in lives of busy everything, to recognise the one equation which would lead them peacefully to what their busy-ness is *supposed* to take them towards, *usually with agitation.* As more people become aware of this equation illustrating interdependent potential, exploration of further possibilities will become a senior component of life to that of busy-ness.

This new age which is so often spoken about as the millennium turns, carries with it a mysterious surge of altruism; many of us discuss our love of humanity whilst exhibiting an abhorrence of people with whom we have regular contact. That old adage stating that *actions speak louder than words* is ever more useful as the physical and personality type urges strive to keep pace with our new mental creativity.

Now, the woman and man analogy described at the beginning of my story*ish* introduction to the main body of this book you are just beginning, is far from perfect, because of the fact that even without the basic 1+1=3 equation which this book seeks to explore, an irreducible element of soul would be apparent. Following the great universal law of correspondence, this is however, another harmonic of the same phenomenon. The woman and man are souls and in joining together in creative aspiration they bring forth into physical life not only a body, but another soul seeking to express itself through earthly existence.

So, 1+1=3, but the combinations are infinite, and I use the equation for illustrative purpose; please do not get too attached to any significance which inevitably will appear throughout what you are reading, and always keep to the forefront of your ponderings, the fact that your interpretations and conclusions will always be senior for you than will be mine.

The child is called *Innominate,* an adjective which I have utilised as a noun, meaning *unnamed,* because I have no wish to reveal a more accurate title or indeed to coin another zippy epithet which loses its usefulness through constant physical repetition without understanding. The word *gestalt* has been used to describe similar *Innominate 1+1=3* type theory, but it has too many psychological connotations for many, to be utilised in today's holistic understanding of the human being and its interdependent potential.

There you have it ... formally introduced to Innominate, who at times we will call *Inno,* pronounced *eeno,* (somewhat confusingly for those of us hailing from the North East of England, as this sound *eeno* is also utilised colloquially to affirm a negative, perhaps followed by the vernacular *pet* or *hinny!*) as we get to know *he* or *she* more intimately ... no ... perhaps *it* is more appropriate for this age of asexual understanding ... set yourself free from a socialisation process you will have endured without doubt, and open yourself up to the dawning of new horizons. Dare to explore with your fellow travellers, that third force which can be built whenever two creators work together. Be willing to fail. Be willing to succeed. Above all else just *be willing* from a viewpoint of *just being*.

I am INNOMINATE. You are INNOMINATE. It is INNOMINATE. What are our responsibilities?

INNOMINATE WENT TO MARKET

Now it may well have been the case that the parents of this child who shall remain nameless, began realising slowly that there may be more to life than they had themselves been told by their parents, but more importantly for the purposes of our story within this book, the child found itself in an environment so at variance with its intuitive aspirations for true human progress, that it almost gagged on its own disappointment. A quantum leap of expectations had occurred it seems, between these generations which brought forth Inno and its parents.

For a short while, let us blend some Cosmology into a portion of Theosophy, mix the results with Rosicrucianism and add a dash of Hinduism; leave to settle for a thought or two before continuing by sprinkling onto the concoction liberal dollops of everything else ever likely to float your way as divine inspiration, including as senior to all else, your own.

The abundant variety which is humanity, is so diverse as to be unfathomable for the embodied mind. Many souls currently being thrust incarnate to this earth as children, seem different to what has gone before. Where have they come from? It is around fifteen centuries since most of the recent births were to be found wandering this earth, at various times of course, given that there are more souls *currently* living with an earthly connection than there ever has been on earth before *in total!* Ponder that statistic the next time you are contemplating solutions to world problems.

Some may have crossed over from that mysterious moon cycle of evolution which went wrong. It is rumoured that Buddha was just such a person. It seems that those who did not quite make it, from an esoteric standpoint, along with their avatars, perhaps a few million years ago, accompanied a rocket like eruption of matter from the depths of the Pacific Ocean into space, and now orbit our planet each month in a lunar cycle. This moon and its life are a deep mystery, but so are the enigmas currently being born.

Venus is to earth what the higher self is to a human being ... does this relationship include the sending of souls for a probable torturous stint of experience and service as earthlings? Do we now have with us souls, last seen during that deeply astral time period of evolution known as Atlantean, now accessing the higher harmonics of Atlantean instinct and desire which we call Aryan intuition and love?

Have the Great Lippika Lords of Karma themselves stepped down their energy to a point of potential incarnation? I do not think such a thing possible, but to cogitate this negative way is itself a throwback to that old practice of socialising a child into being manageable. We here explore the unmanageable! The hitherto unimaginable! We seek the inspiration! We shun the limitations! We fathom the depths and soar to heights of potential seemingly intangible even from a Venusian standpoint.

Who on earth are we?

Innominate did not ask this question until the personality oriented periods of puberty and adolescence were well behind it ... then it was time for work and the personal inquisition had to be satisfied. The market place was still based upon capitalist trading strategies ... people starved whilst food was destroyed in the name of mercantile stability for the few. Innominate was introduced to Nationalism and repelled it. The Global Village which had been distantly heard through a youthful understanding, was manifesting as only a harsher, aberrative and devious domination of the weak by the strong, and not an interdependence of all earthly States and Beings, at which that understanding had hinted.

"We can continue this way, or change," stated Inno on its platform. But the world continued to revolve and only a few agreed. Even those who agreed, disagreed amongst themselves. Time went on and more people joined in. The Aquarian verve finally grew stronger than the Piscean activity which it was designed to supersede. "This was the key," thought Innominate, "it is not from where we all came into this earthly existence that is important, but how we manage ourselves whilst here."

It looked over some of humanity's golden rules to seek sagacity from which to exert a modus operandi suitable for maximum effect in a human lifetime ... Egyptian Wisdom Literature stated that it is wise to thank another in advance for what may be done and parry a blow before it arrives. Brahmanism urged doing nothing to others which would cause you to pay if done to yourself. Buddhism said not to harm others in ways that you would find hurtful. Confucianism confusingly stated that in a spirit of loving kindness one should do unto others what one would *not* have them do to you. Taoism wisely encouraged a law of correspondence with one's neighbour. Judaism stated simply not to do unto your fellow human what you would find hateful to yourself. Christianity said oddly, all things whatsoever ye would that men should do to you, do ye even so to them, for this is the Law and the Prophets. Islam stated that not one of us is a believer until we desire for our brothers what we desire for ourselves. Zoroastrianism says that man is good only when he is willing not to do to another whatever is not good for himself.

So, I have studied all of the above as have you now, *us Innominates,* and I venture that it is time to place all reverence to what has passed on the scrapheap of life that was and start again from a new plateau built from all the good that has gone before. THAT which is called God by the Christians, Jehovah by the Jews, Ultimate Reality by the Hindus, The Buddha Mind by Buddhists, Allah by the Mohammedans and which the Chinese call Tao, THAT IS THE REAL SELF, is all pervading, and may we all experience THAT!

This book is what happens when THAT and THAT meet with an intention to further create THAT ...

Innominate can describe THAT

... if you are continuously externally oriented you may never perceive THAT, and forever find yourself seeking to interdepend with *this or the other,* rather than an additional THAT. Human beings always accomplish eventually what they set out to achieve; you must therefore know exactly what it is with which you are seeking to make contact. Firstly you must connect with yourself. That THAT, before seeking to interdepend with another THAT.

THAT is what this book is about. Just THAT.

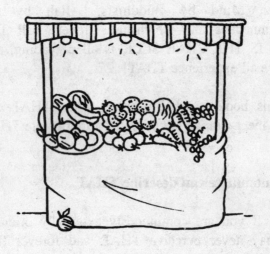

AN ATOM A HUMAN AND THE PLANET
A Little About Radiation

As I composed this contribution to YOU AND ME MAKE THREE, many thousands of people were demonstrating in Germany against a transportation of nuclear waste from one part of their country to another. It seems that they were afraid of nuclear energy potential. Some were fearful of radiation leaks, yet those same people were tearing up railway lines, blocking roads and trying fair means and foul to endanger the transportation of this cargo, the result of which could be just that radiation leakage they were seeking to prevent. Inno found this difficult to comprehend even though it was very cognisant about human nature.

These demonstrators may well feel that it is only themselves who are timorous regarding mismanagement of nuclear energy, but in that supposition they would be very much mistaken. Perhaps they feel that it is only by making such physical demonstrations of their discontent that something will be accomplished to their advantage.

Well, I am thankful for their efforts, as I am to the women of Greenham Common, all those people who mount massive, passive offences whenever a new road is just about to begin construction, the suffragettes, the government that passed a law when the motor car first appeared demanding that a person ran in front of such vehicles waving a red flag, those who spoke of the dangers concerning rail travel at 15 miles per hour, people who ventured the viewpoint in the early days of aeroplanes that, if God had wanted us to fly he would have given us wings … I could cite many more examples but the atmosphere has been created.

Nuclear energy is here to stay and it would be better to work with it rather than against it. How do I know this? Because it is a well foreseen part of human evolution. If the planetary population was almost wiped out tomorrow, along with the art of fire-making, and six year old Joey emerged from a cave four years later with no knowledge of fire, he would discover it within days. Why? Because that divine capacity of fire in man is available, and the physical fires we light daily are merely a lower harmonic of the divine fire capacity within each of us. Fire would exist as inspiration waiting to be cognited upon, and Joey would indeed cognite upon it through necessity. So it is now with nuclear energy.

Telephones, television, radio, the Internet, speedy

travel and indeed anything physically manifested and visible to earthly eyes, was firstly thought ... but what happens before thought? Before the beginning of anything is a thought, but from where is that thought inspired?

We can say that soul contact is a point of inspiration and that would be correct. Physical life to a soul is akin to death for a physical body. The soul during incarnation, enters a kind of suspended animation, or meditation, until awoken by a pathway carved out towards it from its life beneath. This is soul contact and, when a soul *can* become the pilot if you encourage it to so do through such connection. It does not work the other way around, but your physical manifestation on earth *is* visible representation of the invisible you, and care should be taken to maximise your incarnate advantage for personal development of an earthly variety.

We talk of radiation in tones normally reserved for nazism, fascism, excrement, leprosy, Aids, and paedophilia ... we do not want to know about it or at best, we demonstrate about it whilst others ignore it and allow it to be dealt with invisibly. Let me throw you a curve from the norm ...

We must aspire to become more radio active as human beings!

Radio activity is a natural product of evolution, whether it be regarding the development of an atom, a human or the planet. Consciousness is evident in all three examples, and we can glean through looking back-over and forwards, insights related to radiation. Nuclear physicists will be able to describe to you in far greater clarity than can I, the activity which is constantly occurring within an atom ... the smallest particle of a chemical element that can take part in a chemical reaction, and the source of nuclear energy.

An atom has a nucleus around which revolves electrons; not much different in fact, to a solar system where can be found planets revolving around a central sun, or indeed the human being where livers, hearts, spleens, lungs, gonads, solar plexuses and brains, hover around the central force of consciousness which is you or I, both perhaps atoms in a greater life as that greater life is an atom in one life beyond it in magnitude.

Each atom of each organ has consciousness, which is merged into the greater consciousness just ahead of it from an occult viewpoint ... and this brings us to the relevance of AN ATOM, A HUMAN AND THE PLANET taking up so much space in YOU AND ME MAKE THREE. Humanity is becoming radio active ... as I have written in earlier work, telephones, telegraphs, televisions, radios and the Internet are but physical manifestations of a power far greater which lies within each of us, mostly untapped, because of our outward fixations on things external.

Telepathy is the senior relation to all of our earthly mass and individual communication methods.

We are radio active but the potential remains stored inside for most of us ... in fact we are creating our own nuclear waste! We discovered the potential inherent within an atom during the first half of the twentieth century, and the inaugural use in which we deployed it was bombing the Japanese cities of Hiroshima and Nagasaki. Some feel that such deployment lessened human suffering for the majority by inflicting uncontrollable radiation on a minority and it is not the purpose of this book to exhibit a viewpoint about that. We are now discovering that same inherent nuclear potential within human beings ... what will we do with it?

This book seeks to explore the interdependent potential which exists in that magical equation I first coined in my introductory personal development book YOU CAN ALWAYS GET WHAT YOU WANT ... **one plus one does make three** ... ponder it, put knowledge of the equation to use in your life and enhance your existence through practical means.

The atom, when split, emits energy as electromagnetic waves or as moving particles. It has been noted that atoms attract and repel other atoms. Similarly, although with the additional capacity for inflow, perhaps comparable to the attraction capacity of an atom, the neo cortex part of a brain, lying over the mammalian layer which in turn covers the reptilian layer, each layer being the result of a stage of human evolution, is the organ capable and available to us for telepathy of an outgoing and incoming capacity. When we use this new facility at our disposal, we become radio active; when we are en rapport with the rest of humanity, each individual consciousness will merge into that greater consciousness which may be called God or not, depending on your viewpoint. When the planet becomes radio active, I predict that the present rounds of human incarnation will have concluded and the planet itself from an occult point of view, will merge with, perhaps the sun.

This is nothing more than evolution, much of which has been foreseen, and many of such predictions have so far been proved correct with physical evidence. In this portion of the book, I have used many universal laws, but most notably the hermetic axiom which states *as above so below; as below so above,* which admirably describes the law of correspondence. In this succinct treatise on human communication potential, you may like to correspond *stages* of telepathy with more physical manifestations ... to help with this let me share with you Alice Bailey's description of this phenomenon from her book called TELEPATHY AND THE ETHERIC VEHICLE ...

> Instinctual telepathy ... train travel, stations everywhere ... telegraph
> Mental telepathy ... ocean travel, ports on the periphery of all lands ... telephone
> Intuitional telepathy ... air travel, landing place ... radio

My understanding of this, is that the instinctual telepathy here described, is conducted from the solar plexus sector of the human body, which was the region for thinking during Atlantean times. Here, a mother may sense danger for an offspring; many of us receive gut feelings in this area. Mental telepathy is mind to mind, or throat to throat, *vishuddha,* if we are to utilise Hindu chakra terms, and this method is increasingly active as I write these words, for many people both cognisant of what is happening, and even more who are not. It may be that one person transmits from the throat, and another, whose throat centre is not active, may receive such communication in the centre which *is* active, namely the solar plexus. It would be stepped down and only the lesser attributes of this communication would be received. Perhaps the throat centre accomplishes this in conjunction with another centre located between the eyes called the ajna centre, commonly known as the third eye. The intuitional telepathy, I feel, is that of soul to soul. My reality is that once this is common occurrence and the human is aware of it, the body will no longer be able to stand such resultant pressure and will disintegrate, perhaps like a split atom.

My purpose here is not to get technical on you, or shroud this inspirational manual with techno-babble. If you are interested in the flavour which carries these words then I recommend further studies elsewhere, and source material which is more adequate, such as the Alice Bailey book already mentioned, along with her many others on which incidentally, no royalties are paid to anyone. I just want to share with you my reality of the association between varying aspects of this world ... *all is one and one is all* ... and what we can do with our potential once cognisant of our inherent capacities. If you want to learn about yourself, study the macrocosm of which you are a microcosm, and vice versa.

Your energy plus the energy of a fellow human being, will result in energy not readily reducible to its constituent elements. It therefore makes sense to interdepend with your fellow pilgrims, and in so doing, with practice and wisdom, the world will become so much brighter for you. Interdependence, does not mean employing someone, or being employed, it is what you do with, and your attitude to, any relationship you may have. You will have certain qualities not available in another; you will find desirable traits in others of which you currently only dream. When you get together, a third force is created which is the sum of the parts, with an added bonus ... the force which has been created through such magic merging, not belonging to any one individual.

Do not be frightened to interdepend, no matter how many times you may have to try before succeeding. Interdependence is but one step removed from total empathy, which is that merging of consciousness resulting from the norm of telepathy. The most evolved members of the races are experimenting, discussing, failing and succeeding with telepathy. It is only the indolent who are lagging behind and they need only a little more concrete proof before throwing themselves headlong into the ether waves of exploration. Don't waste too much time demonstrating against the nuclear industry ... it needs just enough negative attention to prevent complacency about safety procedures ... explore the positive aspects of radiation ... become radio active yourself.

If you have to ponder nuclear waste begin in your own back yard, for nuclear waste is only the squandering of your telepathic potential through laziness, cynicism, ignorance or habit. That is what I am protesting about!

INNO VISITS DEATH

Why is it that so many of us are petrified of death? I can comprehend and share an apprehension concerning painful dying, but death itself is such a normal part of life that I wonder just how it has carved out a niche for itself as a house of horrors type mystery for us.

"You have not lived until you have died," said Inno, "what we call life is akin to death for our souls, and what we call death is normal life for our souls; quite how we have mixed these concepts into a weird conglomerate of all erroneous answers that have preceded wise pondering of the subject I do not understand."

"How do you know?" I asked Inno, aware that many of us who are free with our groovy and mystical answers to life's questions, frequently freeze when confronted with a direct question.

"Because I visit death daily;" answered Inno, pleased that I had confronted the issue so bluntly, "every time I close my eyes and commune with myself in my inner world of thought, I visit the same place as lives death. To pre-empt your next question which will be along the lines of ... *but how do you really know* ... I know because I am also aware of many previous deaths to this incarnation, and also quite a few between lives moments of recallable consciousness. So, unless you wish to explain my own innate knowingness away with some kind of psycho-babble thought up by a totally psychologically oriented professor of God knows what, believe me ... just believe me. Regarding yourself, I cannot vouch for death as far as your universe is concerned; you must do that personally!"

"Are there any tangible illustrations you can offer me for the purpose of clarification regarding consciousness continuing after death," I asked.

"Apoptosis!" answered Inno succinctly, before continuing in explanation, "the controlled death of cells as part of an organism's normal growth and development; the word is formed from the Greek *apo* and *ptosis*, which together mean *falling off*. There is an understanding within life, other than the complete human, that death is an important part of living, and that *the whole* is more important than its constituent parts. An apoptotic approach to life contains such understanding.

Programmed cell death is a significant part of human embryonic growth. A huge number of nerve cells die during the development of the nervous system for instance. Initially, our digits are not dissimilar to a duck's webbed feet; apoptosis occurs causing cell death in the regions between them during normal development of a limb. Half of all neurons which migrate into our limbs from the spinal cord to connect with our muscles also die. In fact all cells carry within themselves an apoptotic suicide, innately, which will lead them to self destruct unless receiving the right signals to not do so! They understand in their own way, that personal death merely enhances the total life process of which they continue to be an integral part, otherwise why would they kill themselves?

If we were able to view euthanasia as a kind of controlled apoptosis of the human cells within a larger planetary whole, would that not make our clinical decisions easier to reach?

Death is an art, but the art of dying has become a dying art!

Without death on this planet, life could not continue, yet we moan about it and shout out our little fears about our little selves perishing from our own little worlds, without much thought for the greater whole ... be that whole the planet, or just a bigger picture of allowing the great universal axiomatic cycle of creation, transformation and destruction to take its course, with you as part of the destruction and another a part of the creation, whilst a few billion others busy themselves with transformation.

We have the legal right to create births but no statutory right to control our own deaths! Bioethicists beware, too much time spent studying birth lends imbalance to the system. Nor do I condone suicide you understand, for death of such nature but hampers the personal development of whoever tries it. Your question amounts to asking for tangible evidence of life after death, and to answer straightforwardly would be to play right into the hands of the linear thought freaks, who think that all can be understood through comprehension along some kind of time line, and that all must be scientifically proved. Well, I agree that all should be proved scientifically, but if the scientists do not ask the right questions, what chance do we have of discovering the answers?

Little or none!

The first question to the forefront of any scientific quest for the answer to life must be ... *what questions can we ask that presently we cannot conceive of* ... ask this question in a group, and 1 + 1 will give us the answer 3. This answer is the one which cannot be conceived of alone, and it is together that we will progress, so let's do it ... let's do it!"

I thanked Inno for its time, unsure as to whether or not an answer to my question of *consciousness after death* proof had in fact been forthcoming. That is the nature of this book however, to pose as many questions, or more, than the answers it presents. That is why it is different. It turns the world upside down and back to front before then asking what can be seen. That is why it is different. It dares to buck the trend and challenges conventional *unconventional* viewpoints. That is why it is different. It involves *you,* draws you in and tells you nothing about yourself, yet invites you to tell yourself! Is that why it is different? Is it?

INNOMINATE GIRDS ITS LOINS

It soon became apparent as the millennium turned, that divine inspiration and resulting information was quickly becoming available for a hasty assault on the honesty potential of humanity, but as Inno delved into a method for disseminating this new idea of *winning through honesty*, it came across sexism, racism and speciesism. When trying to help and understand, it discovered that sexists were not necessarily racist, speciesists were frequently neither of the other two and, in short, the combinations of *ists* and *isms* seemed infinite, but none necessarily beneficial in the short term for those suffering abuse!

Females thankfully gained equality with males, by forming women's groups which paradoxically excluded men, for the purpose of ensuring that men could not continue to do the same. Black minorities challenged white exclusiveness and at last won equality, which saw one of their first actions being the absurd formation of black only groups. Mixtures of all racial and sexual combinations fought each other, yet combined to fight for animal rights, calling exploitation of our third kingdom, *speciesism*.

The most nonsensical aphorism ever coined, was that stating … *all human beings are created equal.* **They are not!** They do not even have equal potential in the short term, and only viewed over the gamut of total evolution will we perhaps be able to agree that *all souls* were created with equal potential. I am not sure even of this however.

A human being creates itself and is forever responsible for its own outflows and inflows, balances of good and bad, divinity and lack of it. In writing this I in no way depreciate that great body of divinity from which we emanated as sparks of God potential without that greater body losing its integrity; fascinating! Make of this what you will, but a basic on all that we contemplate and do, must be *honesty,* if we are to realise an initiation into our next level of advanced human potential. So by all means challenge all inequalities, but let she, he or it who is without sin cast the first stone, for if we were all honest there would be far less need to fight against inequalities; they would inherently be redressed within a truthful world.

Until we arrive at this integrity, which must

firstly flower within each and every one of us individually, let those who passionately seek equality in one department of life, also seek it for others in departments for which they presently have little or no interest. Let the vegan speak kind words on behalf of the white person who has just had land confiscated during a black majority uprising in Africa, whilst also upholding the rights of those blacks unfairly confiscating such land, when white majorities elsewhere crush their blooming aspirations. Let the feminist protect the violations of male rights whatever they may be, and vice versa; whilst all this interplay is occurring, the challenge is that of maintaining and developing honesty.

Inno girded its loins.

"Being liked or disliked is but a personality oriented reaction of others to oneself; if one is honest then the colour of affection matters not. Soul quality and the exoteric manifestation of it through a vision and execution of that vision, is on what I shall base my life. Honesty is contacting the soul, and remaining true to the purpose of that soul, through the vehicle of a personality."

Innominate's loins were girded.

INNO ENCOUNTERS TECHNOLOGY

The middle aged lady was asked if she used the Internet … "whatever happened to a good old chat over the garden fence," she replied, "no I don't!" Innominate intervened with a comment … "garden fence chats were more common when we were fighting two world wars weren't they. Our mothers and fathers were comfortable with that type of communication, but such conversations were frequently pure gossip. Neighbourliness was often synonymous with nosiness, and the friendly little town centre was rarely stocked with the needs of modern western living."

Such comments as were those emanating from this entity known as Inno did not fit the frame of the discussion in which it was partaking. I empathise with Innominate; in my own flirtations with new age groups and more general activities I am frequently confronted with romantically melancholic visions of the past, and how *others have it right* whilst us humans living a modern western style life always seem to *get it wrong!* When discussing the earth and our general environmental challenges, my thoughts are often turned by others to beautiful visions of aboriginal living, apache relationships with animals and birds, tribes which live high in the Andes mountains and warn us of impending ecological doom, but rarely to the successes which our own societies are offering.

I hear loud moans about the motor car and water wastage; the analogies with primitive cultures I now find to be totally uninspirational through overuse. Those constantly griping about the way we abuse the land and comprehensively take all without giving anything, are usually to be seen as are most of us, driving cars, shopping at supermarkets, taking regular baths and sprinkling the lawn, despite fears of water shortages, watching television, and in general ... *well, I think you get the picture*. My invitation to such people, when their griping is scraping away at my very beingness, is requesting them to give it all up and *live the stories they are telling* as more beautiful than *the stories which we are living!*

If you think that world hunger can be cured by travelling backwards in time to primitive means you are in fact mistaken. If you disagree with me then do write and tell how this can be accomplished! If you feel that the world is suddenly about to give up the motor car, tele-anything, comfortable living, easy shopping, safe housing, warmth, predictable food supplies, and all else the west seems to be accused of, then think also of the consequences. The six billion or so incarnate souls currently wandering this planet are more numerous than the sum total of all souls incarnated on earth ever! That is part of evolution.

You cannot feed progress by stepping backwards.

The POSITIVE ATTITUDE CLUB type philosophy which both myself and Inno embrace, is of the aikido variety, where all energy is transmuted to benefit, which for our purpose here is humanity. You would also find that those primitive civilisations to which we attach romantic notions of nostalgic aspiration, predominantly endeavour themselves towards that which we have and are. If you give a Hottentot the opportunity, once educated in the benefits of our civilisation, to adopt some of our western style advantages, they invariably will accept. The American Indian, Aboriginals, Peruvian tribes, Brazilian jungle people and Pygmies have all now seen the benefits of a life saving shot of anti-biotic for a family member who otherwise would have died. Those suffering nostalgia for earlier western culture should also spare a thought for past child mortality, hunger deprivation and depravation that seems to disappear when wandering in mental retrospect through past glorious avenues.

I watched a fascinating survival type programme about Indonesian Head-hunters, and their harmony with nature and most especially their immediate surroundings. It was extremely impressive. The tribal leader was not able to contribute to the programme however as he was serving a goal sentence for having taken a human head only four years earlier!

The 1+1=3 equation is so obvious here that I initially sought complicated means to describe it before abandoning them in favour of simplicity. The good of the past plus the good of our primitive cultures, when added to modern technology and progress, equals a win for all and a massive expansion of earthly synergy. We can learn from all cultures, but it need not be at the expense of our own. That is 1 - 1 + 1 = 1, or, stagnation before an inevitable collapse of all that we have worked throughout the millennia to achieve.

If you must have nostalgia, then let it be for the future, but only once you are capable of living in the moment!

One evening we were discussing Dolly the freshly 1997 cloned sheep. This conversation was supposed to last around fifteen minutes as an introduction to an evening on telepathy and the need for altruistic love during its exercise, despite all differences we have with one another. It was a most inspiring evening, especially when discussing any role the soul would have to play in such clones, *(think about that for a moment)* and we never did get to the designated subject that evening. When our conversation turned to the ethics of cloning, I was alone in voicing the fact that such progress is unstoppable. Whether we like it or not it will happen, and energy spent bemoaning this aspect of evolution would be better spent using mental aikido ... in other words, how can this energy benefit us?

Just as physical fire became available for discovery when the divine aspect formed part of our planetary energy influx, so too does our capacity to control conception arrive within our creative domain, when relevant divine, and in this case Aquarian energy, is focused in our direction, arriving as part of what I have called THE SEVEN BEAMS FROM OUTER SPACE VIA THE MILKY WAY, which power every mien of known planetary life.

Cloning en masse, arrived in the 1980's along with home computers. Suddenly we were able to replicate huge chunks of data ... not copy, but clone you understand; there is a difference. Cloning is an exact duplication of the parent, be that parent human or a datum. Music was introduced to the digital domain, or vice versa, and of course cloning became possible in that art. I have done it myself on albums which I recorded during the 1990's. Most of my songs contain four part harmonies; I would multi track each part several times and this produces a rich blend and excellent effect. It is also very time consuming, so I would record only one chorus for instance, and *fly* that chorus into the song wherever it was needed.

There is no drop in sound quality because it is a clone! Some think it is cheating, but if we work *with* this potential, it eventually becomes assimilated into the working musical environment.

So too with human cloning ... it will come, mark my words, and if we work with it, rather than antagonistically against it, although it must be said that our human comportments require a certain amount of protest and demonstration to draw our attention towards negative capacities, that we do not run away with our own power, synergy will prevail to our advantage, and something new and enlightening will arrive on our mutual path inviting us to walk a little further.

The advantages of cloning are vast, but I am afraid currently, politically incorrect in all but the most liberal of circles, for the purpose of discussing the refinement of our races. Through cloning we could produce human bodies so fine and rare, that it would be with ease that many of us would be able to access planes so far in advance of our awareness because of the limitation our dense bodies produce, and consequent grounding, that we may perhaps even be able to glimpse heaven whilst walking through hell! We are still too close to memories of Nazi Germany for lengthy exploration of this capacity however, when such potential was reeked against the world for the purpose of producing advantage for only one nation. Please do not think for a moment that I am discussing the same thing here, and nor am I suggesting that the human race is ready for this test. It certainly was not ready during the 1939-1945 portion of the twentieth century world war! It seems however, that human cloning is imminent, and we must prepare ourselves mentally and physically, if we are not to find ourselves talking about the good old days, which were never quite as good as they seem during reflection.

The most explosive equation in history is now upon us; we can utilise it for the mass benefit of humanity through progress, charity and love, or let it slip into the hands of the few who forever seek to destroy our true potential. We *must* utilise it for good, because without doubt there are those who will use it in evil, and for this reason we must gain a head start! You, me and the rest of us …

INNO'S MISSION

"Spirituality begins, where religions dare not tread," began Inno in answer to my question as to what was its function in life, "and my *reason for being* is *remaining faithful to my mission*. This mission lies behind all that I do and say; it is senior to all goals that I aspire towards, for it is through my mission that I know what goals to set for myself. This is in line with the theme behind your book called THE 49 STEPS TO A BRIGHT LIFE, where you state that …

this world is not made from atoms … it is built with stories

… the stories you urge people to find within themselves are what I, and yourself elsewhere in your writings, call missions. Each of us will find, if we spend the time searching, a unique theme within ourselves which we can relate through living …"

"Most of us are too busy *being busy* to actually find the one aspect of life for which we are actually searching," I added.

"That is correct," continued Inno, "and I think that you here speak about HAPPINESS, that elusive state which many of us erroneously believe can exist as an entity in itself. As you well know however, it is a by-product of living your story, or mission …"

"Happiness arrives during the accomplishment of an otherwise unrelated goal," I interrupted, risking a quotation from another of my books.

"Couldn't have put it better myself," congratulated Inno, without reference to personal indulgence in my own work, "the thing is however, that so much literature now exists in the world of personal development, self help, personal psychology or whatever you wish to call it, that people have now become addicted to the latest ways to discover their own missions … the problem is that they never find out what their personal stories are, because they are too busy looking for them, filling out forms and staking claims as adherents to whomsoever is the latest fashionable personal development guru on the block.

Discovering your story is not an external process … it can only be found within. No amount of form filling will prepare you for that exploration. Such expeditions inside ourselves require persistence, peace, quiet, dignity and a degree of solitude. I therefore urge everyone away from the bureaucratic approach found in many books and seminars, and towards their inner worlds, for existing in these places are unique stories just waiting to be told. There is nothing greater in life than telling your own story through living."

"What is your mission Inno," I asked.

"The processes which occur between you, myself and the readers, best illustrate my mission, for it is easy to compose words in a fanciful expression for the purpose of wowing all that ask, but it is more honest to show by results what your mission is. So, if you want to know how successful I am with my mission, then ask yourself if I have helped you; ask your readers if our little chats have inspired them, and should the answers be more affirmative than negative, then that is the exact ratio of accomplishment to failure which currently exists within my mission. The mission in action is senior to relating my mission statement to you.

Individual episodes of success or failure do not affect my happiness however, for happiness exists merely through an association with my personal mission, and is only tempered by alignment or lack of alignment with this mission. Goals, objectives and dreams come and go, but the mission remains the same. Find the mission and you find that vertical alignment with your soul purpose. You cannot fill out a form for that now can you?"

I did not answer the question, for it was plain that I understood all that Inno had said to me. I once again thanked it for affording me time, ever more grateful that such an attractive mission as Inno's had found its way as an influence into my own life.

Without a mission and not knowing what story you wish to tell through living, us human beings have no self appointed direction in life. If you do not make contact with your mission through spending time with yourself alone for that purpose, then at best you will become part of someone else's mission, for any purpose is better than no purpose is it not? Your fulfilment as only part of someone else's plans will be minimal however, unless such a course of action is your actual mission, which I doubt. There are leaders and followers, neither being innately senior to the other. Successful followers however, are firstly, on purpose and knowledgeable of their personal missions, and secondly following only as part of that mission.

So, no more forms no more hints, just spend time on what it is you should be doing; that is your mission. A little attention spent each day in meditation or relaxation, alone and in peace, quiet and creative space, should do the trick. Then again it might not; its up to you!

DON'T CHANGE NUTTIN
For The First Little While

In my heart, PeRFECT WORDS and MUSIC began at the end of the 1960's. In effect, it came into physical being whilst the Murray Family lived in America during the late 1980's, by 1993 it had become a limited company, and 1996 saw the inclusion of INTERNATIONAL into the title, and the addition of a dynamic new partner to our fold, who helped us launch our products into the Russian speaking countries, along with expansion through translations into many other languages.

With each step of progress in connection with any type of expansion, comes a surge of energy. People who know themselves and have honourable intentions, utilise this energy for good in the main, and often bad when they cease knowingly exercising a *will to good*. Other people become involved in certain situations and the overwhelming desire seems to be towards change of any type.

People like to stamp their personalities onto whatever circumstances in which they happen to be involved. In the case of PeRFECT WORDS and MUSIC, the trend was to remove me from the workaday world of commerce, and shut me up in some Ivory Tower to inspire the words which my colleagues could then sell. It took little persuasion from them I must affirm, but that had not been my initial intention I should also admit.

The problem of having me around the company offices lay in the area of change, or to be more accurate, how my colleagues perceived the course that necessary change should take. I had been at the helm for the duration of the company's lifetime, and it had been run with too much heart and not enough head; there was an imbalance so to speak, and I was happy for that lack of alignment to be addressed. I watched the transformation by helping wherever I could, but it seemed that the most benefit could be achieved from my retaining an exterior viewpoint.

As I am the founder of THE POSITIVE ATTITUDE CLUB, and the author of inspirational books that applaud progress, initiative and achievement, it was with some reserve that I presented my recommendation to the board, knowing full well that it could leave me looking sour and rejected, which was certainly not the case.

"Don't change nuttin," was my suggestion as a golden rule, delivered in the American vernacular, "and once you have checked stability follow the three lesser rules for business transformation regarding sales … 1 promote. 2 promote. 3 promote!

These rules exist for any aspects of life undergoing a similar set of circumstances. Personally, whenever I was to undertake a new project or perhaps a television appearance, my immediate concern years ago would have been to buy some new clothes, get a haircut, change my diet to that of the surrounding in which I found myself, and generally remove myself from items of familiarity. I now acknowledge such behaviour as a mistake. Attention which is required for the subject in which you should be involved, is diverted from where it should be, to the new jacket and how it hangs, the haircut which is too short, the coffee induced caffeine shakes which do not usually affect you as your coffee consumption is normally regulated, the lack of sleep and the draining effect it has had on you because our hotel bed was strange … I could continue but the picture has been painted.

Don't change nuttin until your situation has stabilised and you are once again *at cause* over it and not *the effect* of it!

My business analogy works well in personal life as it does for all aspects of living. I listened to the criticisms of what had gone before at PeRFECT

WORDS and MUSIC, without any intrusion from my ego, over which I am now well in control after years of exploration resulting in much failure and many successes, and as I listened, I wondered how the business had lasted beyond a week from conception.

The invoices had been too flowery, wordy and literate ... *obviously inspired by an author* ... there had been lots of attention on decor and atmosphere ... *obviously inspired by an artist* ... there had been an out of financial ratio involvement with the recording studio ... *obviously inspired by a musician* ... an abundance of direction about how to handle communications with respect ... *obviously inspired by a love of people as leader of the PAC* ... a request for peace and quiet ... *obviously inspired by an understanding of meditation.*

We employed someone who left a bacon and mushroom pasty in the refrigerator, knowing full well that we had an agreement about our environment being a meat free zone. This same person, when paid a week early because of Christmas time, which we do not celebrate, then asked if she could have her money even earlier so that the money could be in the bank by that earlier date which was on the cheque. The temptation is to give way to these simple little requests but we became stronger through experience and did not.

Don't change nuttin until you are able to understand the wisdom innate in every aspect of all situations which allowed your presence to occur in the first place.

When you have stabilised, then instigate changes with economy, and note any egotistical urges which may sway your judgement away from the objectives and goals. As your power increases through attention to these simple rules, so too can your changes accelerate.

Change for change sake equals ego involvement.

Don't fool yourself that you are above emotion, ego, personality, and this material world, if you find yourself making willy nilly changes according to your moods, temperament and tastes.

Treading warily equals treading boldly ... successfully!

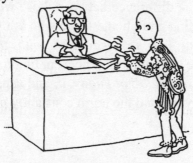

INNOMINATE AND THE MANDALA

Talk of not changing things when taking over a business or indeed any aspect of life until aware of much that has gone before, set Inno thinking about its new obsession ... *the way that all of its newly acquired friends were handling what universally has come to be known as The New Age Of Aquarius.*

It had twice lived in the solid confines of the previous Piscean Age, which had lasted as do all major astrological periods, for around two thousand years, and was aware that despite having no personal affinity for the building of churches, separative religions, wars, or indeed almost any aspect of pisceanism, most of this past history had been a necessary part of our planetary mythology.

There now seemed to be a definitive split in humanity, illustrated limply in the occident and orient, by the difference between those who are seen to be attending church and those who know that they have but to live *in meditation with the soul* to discover the church of their heaven. Innominate knew this, *because it had not known it,* and aspired to find out what lay beyond the norm constantly presented to it.

In its earlier years, the mistakes of youth had seen Inno discussing human potential with those not able to contemplate it, for they still lived within the solidity of piscean energy which told them that there was no potential beyond what they could see physically, unless they joined up devotionally with a building or a monument or a congregation or any of many other old ways; what now alarmed it was the fact that Innominate's modern associates frequently demonstrated equally narrow viewpoints from their new *new age* perspectives.

Apparently nothing had changed!

If this continues, thought Innominate, *the beam from outer space carrying this fresh influx of faster vibrating love energy, will merely furnish varied and stronger desires within humankind.* Something had to be done about this lack of mental calibration in the habits of the human subjects for this descending cosmic phenomenon.

In its early twenties, Innominate had wandered the divine potentials available at that time, and in so doing suffered the suppression of contemporary religions. During the 1960's, Inno's saviour had been waiting for a visit from it, in an old book shop not far from London's Trafalgar Square. Now, this was no ordinary book shop, for it was very old and specialised only in the metaphysical, esoteric, mystical and generally philosophical type of material. It was surprisingly well patronised by those who did not consider it a burden to travel all day for the purpose of availing themselves of this truly magnificent inspirational material.

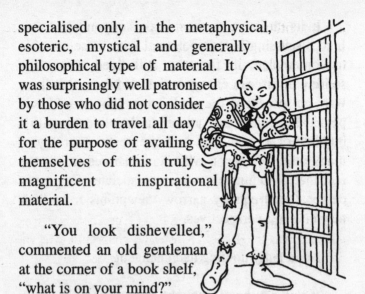

"You look dishevelled," commented an old gentleman at the corner of a book shelf, "what is on your mind?"

Innominate looked surprised, "how can you tell that there is something on my mind, and who are you, if you do not mind me asking?"

"If it comforts you to give me a name call me John W, but actually like yourself, I have no name, merely a purpose."

"A purpose, and what can that be; it must include me in some way as you seem to know so much about me?"

"It includes you, but not as some special being apart from the rest of your human associates. You and I are of similar paths, but perhaps I have trodden mine a few centuries longer than have you yours. You are in a sacred place my friend; you stand on a spot that I have personally witnessed bearing the weight also of Krishnamurti and his brother, Alice and Foster Bailey, Annie Besant before she became a Theosophist, Bishop Leadbeater before he adopted that title, Max Heindel ... I witnessed Madame Blavatsky grumbling at her assistant as she fumbled, much preoccupied, through five books at once whilst smoking a self rolled cigarette, I have seen the auras of ascended initiates occupying that same spot. KH was there, as was the Tibetan Master Djwhal Khul, Morya, and I saw Jesus there on more than one occasion.

You look shocked Innominate; do not be! This meeting with me is most fortuitous for you and me both, for I have your next step with which it is my purpose to serve you, and you are in a position to receive it, which undoubtedly is your purpose and a help to your mission, so everyone wins in this instance, which is not always the case it must be said. Latterly standing on that same spot I have noticed a very different group of people; Claude Bristol talked with Harold Sherman there, about James Allen who had been on that same spot 40 years before, although unbeknownst to them; Napoleon Hill argued with W Clement Stone before both retired for a cup of tea in that café opposite. Just a few years ago there was an influx of many Americans who confused the character and soulful wisdom available from these shelves with the personality whims, caprices and desires of humanity for which such illumination is not intended.

Yes, it is indeed a sacred spot, and I have for you something which is your next step on this rickety path, *to where,* no one is exactly sure!"

The old man handed a piece of crumpled parchment to Innominate, whose mouth was open showing signs of startlement by that time. What appeared on that parchment is now printed here for you in this book, as an indication that no matter what path you follow, all lead to but one holy place. It is the following of this path, which we call life, and the purpose for such a path we can but speculate upon, sometimes quite accurately I feel.

A Mandala, is a symbolic circular figure representing the universe in various religions; in psychology, such a symbol in a dream, represents the dreamer's search for completeness and self-unity. The word comes from the Sanskrit *mándala,* meaning *disc.* For Innominate, it represented a chance to transcend through understanding, all in which he had become enmeshed through trying to comprehend life through religion, with only piscean interpretations for guidance.

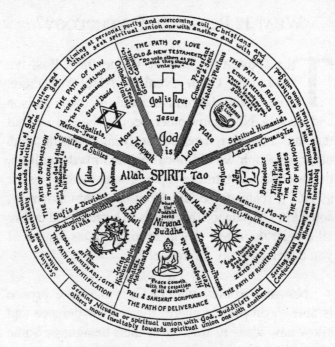

Mandala of the Eight Paths

"Now," continued the old man, "what you do with the new understanding which undoubtedly will come your way through this Mandala, is for you to decide, but you stood on that sacred spot as had those before you, and as will many in times to come; in so doing you began a process from which it is impossible to escape."

Innominate thanked the old man and returned home.

What Is Personal Psychology?

The above title was the theme for a POSITIVE ATTITUDE CLUB evening. Nico was there, Ginger too, Innominate, and of course Allison and myself. Not many other people showed up, but that has not ever deterred us from inspiring each other, although we did once feel and maybe still do, that when around thirty people present themselves for a PAC, it seems to be just about the right amount for some kind of balance that needs to be achieved before all can *let their hair down,* so to speak, as it were, if you understand my inference!

Now the problem with PACs is that not everyone is able to drop their guard, lower their defence and allow new ideas to wash over their beingness. Some of us still feel that *we are* whatever data has just been assimilated by *the intellect,* and this can impair potential when inspiration is sought. I experimented by printing out a welcome form which invited participants to write down what the title meant to them, with a note asking readers to not turn over the form, thereby keeping secret what was on the other side. Of course everyone did, and this was our first insight into one tiny weenie little aspect of psychology, but the one on which the vast majority of the world is fixated. That old materialistic approach to the subject which invariably struggles with neuroses and just how us humans react to our environment.

On the reverse was a sticker ... I asked how many F's each of us could see ... try it quickly now ...

> PHOTOGRAPHS OF OUR
> FAMILY AND FRIENDS
> REMIND US OF EVENTS
> SO WE HAVE FIRM
> MEMORIES OF THE PAST

... there were three divergent answers, all incorrect, and my purpose for the exercise was to illustrate that we all perceive life differently. 3, was the most common perception, followed by 4 and 5. In fact there are 6 F's, and this was judged an enjoyable practical exercise; yet, it is just another trick of the personal development trade some call personal psychology, which doesn't get us anywhere else other than that mental place already described by me as *where we all perceive life differently.* Earth!

We continued and each of us read out aloud our understanding of the subject; these readings consisted of clever replies, questioning answers and even nothing. It transpired that there were as many definitions of the title as there were people in that room, just as I had expected. Unfortunately for clever Dick me, I invited Nico to relate his understanding of the subject before I was able to reveal mine. Our understandings were more or less identical bar an interpretation of the *ology* aspect of the word psych*ology*. A tactical blunder that would have been were we in a Brownie points situation which we were not. If inspiration is forthcoming it matters not from where, unless the tiresome little personality based ego is involved that is, which mine is not.

The word *psychology* is derived from the Greek word *psukhē* meaning breath, life or soul ... perhaps even all three ... and the suffix *ology,* signifying *the study of,* which Nico understood as *knowledge of.* An insignificant nuance you may feel, but important to me, as my understanding was more active and Nico's more of a fait accompli. I am sure it amounted to the same thing overall, but my definition powered me to further understanding, whereas the mere *knowledge of the soul,* as a definition would have left me not actively seeking it. I don't want to get too complicated here, and will leave it at that and hope you follow my meaning.

So, there we were, in a forum designed for inspiration; but the subject was unfortunately one also being studied elsewhere by a lady who was present. This person literally spent the whole evening defending her studies ... not that anyone had attacked them you understand. It was just that the majority present felt that there was undue concentration within our society on the materialistic aspect of psychology where study stops at humanity's personality reactions, and not enough, as already mentioned, on studying the soul, which, if studied long and hard enough in all the right places, will be scientifically proved as existing, according to an early twentieth century clairvoyant.

I mentioned psycho surgery, a subject on which I am deemed opinionated. A tough tag to accept for one who boasts aspirations of living without beliefs and opinions. Okay, I am against it, and may that be one of the last convictions to leave me before I find myself in that paradisiacal world I feel exists just around the corner, where judgements have ceased to be necessary.

I talked animatedly about pushing 10,000 volts between the temples of a human being *just to see what happens,* lunging an ice pick up underneath a person's eye to hack at whatever is there, *just to see what happens,* and sawing into someone's skull in order to swing what looks like a butter knife at bits of brain, and not stopping until the patient becomes incoherent, *just to see what happens* ... yes the patient would be conscious in that particular example!

What about rendering a pubescent female infertile so that she cannot breed, after declaring her a moron because she does not respond to life as *you* would wish her to so do! Instead, why not dig into the consciousness of a culture and question why it still gallingly circumcises its females ... or try asking America why it still needlessly and cruelly circumcises its males. How is psychology helping us respond to living as souls having a human experience? Like this, by constant referral to the animal origins of the human body, in ignorance of the spiritual spark which allows us to be self conscious and look at the way we think?

If you can't get 'em in the socialisation box,

electrocute them, cut them, psycho-babble them, certify them, criminalise them and humiliate them ... easy isn't it! If we do it efficiently enough we will create a society which I analogise to the compression of an audio signal, thus making it suitable for television transmission ... all the highs and lows are pushed into a narrow wave band so as not to upset the inferior television speaker systems most of us suffer. This is what we are doing to all those people who do not see life as does the majority. Slowly but surely, it will transpire however, that the bright amongst the psychology fraternity, will acknowledge certain traits and destigmatise them, like dyslexia, and such things may even become aberrantly fashionable for a while! But only those cognisant within their studies, of man as a spiritual being, will be capable of such investigation, let alone success.

I was accused of presenting an imbalanced viewpoint and was thankful for the compliment. We were evidently on a downward slide and it was suggested that we were concentrating on the negative. Now, this has frequently been the case argued whenever unpleasant issues have raised themselves. I regularly affirm and will take the opportunity to so do here, that *positive* in POSITIVE ATTITUDE CLUB is nothing to do with the actual thinking process, rather it relates to your position when thought occurs. I think it possible to *live* positively when you are behind your thought mechanism ... thinking them rather than you being thought by them. That is what my definition of a positive attitude is, and I was most definitely positive that night of the psychology kuffuffle.

Try as we might, we were unable to stabilise that conversation onto personal psychology as being the path to one's soul. We touched on it, there was a diagram on the blackboard illustrating it, but it just seems that most were happy to concentrate on the subject from a materialistic angle, and there is nothing wrong with this ... it is one tiny weenie little aspect of psychology, as I have already mentioned. If we concentrate too much on it however, we may forget about humanity's true potential.

I related the story about a friend of mine with whom I had acted during the 1980's. I bumped into him again at the beginning of the 90's and asked what he was then doing. He was very posh and always had been, with an English upper class air about himself, and he told me that he was currently trading on those qualities from rooms in London's Harley Street as a psychiatrist.

"Are you qualified?" I asked naively.

"Of course not," began the reply, "I know nothing about the subject. I am an actor and my patients are quite happy after they have been with me ... they are unaware of any difference between me and one who has studied text books for years!"

Now this did interest me, because when I enquired further, allowing for his ego and consequent exaggerations, it transpired that he was achieving excellent results. Just by listening! The fact that he had become a con man was secondary to the fact that he was genuinely helping many.

I also mentioned during the evening, that as an audio producer, I had produced ten long and boring psychology educational lectures written and presented by two chief examiners for a particular examination board used by many schools and colleges. Naturally I was interested in what they had to say, as I was, in addition to producing at that time, writing one of my earlier books. I was shocked to find that they knew almost nothing about human beings and just about everything concerning text book psychology ... the quotations rolled of their tongues as they had done habitually, year after year, to succeeding classes of unwitting students, unable themselves to distinguish between data and wisdom, or lack of it!

If we as a society, continue to concentrate on what is presented to us, rather than consistently looking behind what we are told for the real truth, then we are doomed to living as automatons ... which incidentally is what psycho surgery, many branches of psychiatry and much of psychology has as a goal ... to make you conform to certain narrow guidelines which *they* can understand. There is no room for a non conformist as it makes the establishment uncomfortable. There is no box in which to place such a person. Just a bin. Where would all the great artists and thinkers of our world be if we allow such behaviour to continue as the norm? The loony bin! Of course this title is politically incorrect so it gets changed from time to time, but the theme remains the same ... there are however, less loonies in the bin then there are loonies in society putting them there.

There is a beautiful and quite moving film which was released in 1995 called DON JUAN DE MARCO, starring Johnny Depp, Marlon Brando and Faye Dunaway. In it, Johnny Depp portrays a character who believes himself to be the legendary lover Don Juan, and Marlon Brando is his psycho analyst, with Faye Dunaway as Brando's wife. It is a wonderful portrayal about a reversal of consciousness, whereby Brando to his joy, eventually sees things Depp's way, by beginning for the first time in his life to live his own story, rather than the one handed on a plate to him by society. Watch it and you may be moved as was I!

So, where do we go from here? Create a PAC of your own and discuss the title WHAT IS PERSONAL PSYCHOLOGY? Question all that is, and if something is not, ask why not. Do not ever be afraid to own a viewpoint outside the narrow constraints of society, for in so doing you are supporting a foundation which I seek here to rock.

Rock it ... rock it!

Innominate Encounters Sanat Kumara

Whatever happened to the doves, oxen and sheep, along with all of the other merchandise that Jesus ordered from that temple in Jerusalem around two thousand years ago? I guess that they were sold elsewhere. The money changers and lenders probably moved just around the corner until the heat died down before inching their way back into the temple, which apparently had taken forty six years to build. Jesus said he would rebuild it in three days, but he was speaking metaphorically by actually describing the planned resurrection as his own temple, but the recipients of his communication took this meaning literally.

Now, I reckon at the time, people who had but caught a glimpse of this great man's sandal would have bragged of their deep friendship with him to those whom such a relationship would impress; perhaps not the Romans of course. Maybe like John W and his recital of all those great people who had stood on that sacred spot where then stood Innominate, there was more of a symbolic lilt to the words of not only Jesus at that time, but many more aspects of current life.

We always seek the actual meaning of everything rather than seeking the poetic, hidden or special meanings which exist in many places for those who dare to look ... daring to contemplate new ways! To me, the resurrection always merely signified the concept that there is real life after corporeal death. That which is obvious and blatant we can call exoteric, like the temple which took forty six years to build, but that which I and many colleagues spend our time exploring is hidden from ordinary view, like your own personal resurrection, for the understanding of far fewer people currently, and we call this esoteric.

Inno was sent a simple new age type brochure which advertised events, therapies, products and personalities. Its eye fell on one such advert which stated that Sanat Kumara would be channelling something or other through a lady, which he incidentally knew from many years prior, into a healing workshop, whatever that may be. Now, Innominate is not cynical, and nor is this writer, we both aspire towards lives free from beliefs, judgements and opinions, but it is impossible as a human being, certainly at my stage of evolution, to let controversial comments, duplicitous adverts, dubious assertions, harmful wild talk and false claims, to go floating off into the ether without further discussion as to their inherent validity.

This guy, thing or energy known in an increasing

number of new and old age circles as Sanat Kumara, is a pretty heavyweight dude, as one might say after watching an American soap. According to this advert which I have just mentioned, Sanat Kumara is described as ... *Planetary Logos.* The offer continues by affirming that *an ascended master will be assigned to each individual throughout the session.*

In actual fact, Sanat Kumara is LORD OF THE WORLD, but do not ask me to prove it, as I will not ask the lady organising the healing workshop to prove that he is our planetary logos, which I feel also to be true! My sources describe Sanat Kumara as ... having a principle of the planetary logos working through him, thus making him a direct incarnation of the planetary logos ... *an expression of his divine consciousness.*

To describe or clarify just what the planetary logos is ... get the idea of your life, and how you hold it in place, with the help of automatic genetics, using a series of ideas, inspirations, evolutionary steps and mental planning. Be aware of just how many things have gone wrong with your life, together with its successes, and then picture an energy similar to that energy which is you but more evolved, holding a planet in its meditations. When you have an accident, you may destroy some body cells. A hiccup in the meditations of the planetary logos, or spirit, would probably result in a catastrophe such as half the planet's oceans drying up. It's an interesting scenario don't you think?

To some, Sanat Kumara is God, whilst to others Sanat Kumara's God, perhaps that great spiritual entity holding the physical sun in its thoughts, is God ... again to others this is all but blasphemy as they continuously prefer to worship an old man with a beard sitting on a throne in the sky treating humanity as humanity treats each other ... *with judgement, opinions and beliefs* ... not a lot to aspire towards there I venture!

Not to labour this point beyond usefulness, the Sanskrit word Kumara is formed from *ku* ... with difficulty ... and *mara* ... mortal. *Living in a dense vehicle on planet earth with difficulty;* well, that does not just describe Sanat Kumara I am sure you will agree. It is interesting that this simple word summarises every single one of us incarnate here on earth at this moment, along with the more general idea of difficulties the rarefied concept of spirit has working through its denser forms of matter.

Innominate knew all of this information, and more. What perturbed it was the fact that during every one of this lady's seminars, according to that advert, the great spiritual energy holding our planet in its meditations, thus allowing our lives to evolve, was to have its attention diverted from whatever it thought this attention should be on, to what this lady has thought up for a workshop. Not content with claiming this power, the lady further attests to the fact that an ascended master will be assigned to each individual throughout the session. Ascended masters which come immediately to mind are Saint Germain and St Paul; although this is not an area of expertise for me, I should imagine that these great beings are quite busy with greater concepts dealing not just with some personalities of humankind, but perhaps with humankind itself. If not, I do hope some one or thing is looking out for us!

So, we now know where God will be on certain given days according to this advert, with which I am not yet quite finished, for it further claims that Sanat

Kumara, *Planetary Logos,* will be *channelling* through this lady for the purposes of a healing workshop. This lady must be awesome, in fact Innominate said that she is, but not in the way I mean, because the channelling of such energy is akin to sending 50,000 volts through a single hair size strand of copper wire ... in other words if it were to happen the woman would frazzle!

There is no such thing as absolute; I use this universal axiom in my defence as I hypocratise my claim of aspiring towards life without beliefs, opinions and judgements ... *I believe* that this lady is no more in touch with Sanat Kumara than am I or any other regular mortal walking this earth ... it is *my opinion* that such claims are damaging to those of us boldly striding forth into an area we call divinity for the purpose of exploration into human potential ... it is *my judgement* that we should ignore such claims and related types of wild talk in the hope that some day we will all be satisfied with the *actual* status which is ours rather than some *fancied* status self bestowed to woo others into one's lair.

Innominate mentioned that it was honest leaving the PAC open to individual interpretation; we discussed the fact that if I were to make wild claims about my own status and abilities, mentioning deceitfully that Sanat Kumara, Saint Germain or St

Paul dropped into physical meetings from time to time, we would have an explosion of PACs around the world stimulated by interest similar to that which followed publicity given to a statue which was seen to cry shedding a real wet tear ... we concluded that this is precisely why we are happy with the steady and sane expansion of contacting people when both we and they are ready.

Innominate wishes to affirm the fact that the lady running these healing workshops is a good person as are we all innately, but it is that which we do with this inherent goodness, separating the good from the not so good.

......

As I wrote these words in April 1997, an experiment began in America to examine statistically, the effectiveness of prayer. I have always associated prayer with a kind of personality request for God to bestow that personality or other personalities with some thing, be it health, a material possession or a state of mind. I differentiate between prayer and meditation personally, by not indulging in the former, and predominantly when taking part in the latter, ensuring it is of the service variety for the general well being of humanity ... *isn't that good of me* ... I added that last superficial cant comment in italics, because that which preceded it seemed on re-reading, pompous, but relevant nevertheless so it will remain.

Let Light and Love and Power restore the Plan on Earth.

This line was critical in attracting me towards the idea of influencing world evolution through meditation. I cannot conceive of a plan to test the efficacy of this meditation statistically, but 1800 patients enduring, *or not,* as the case may be, heart surgery, are to be tested over a two year period to examine the power of prayer ... 600 will be prayed for and told about it ... 600 will be prayed for and not told about it ... 600 will not be prayed for.

The statisticians describe the potentially far more powerful prayer of the loved ones for all those taking part as *background noise!* So, if those who are prayed for and know about it do well, the power of human minds will be at work, and or the placebo effect ... if those who are prayed for and do not know about it do well, God will have intervened ... if those who are not prayed for and either know about it or not do well, it is my supposition that the totality of divinity and the power of the mind will be in question ... *by the statisticians that is!*

Does it ever cross your mind that humanity is

obsessed with a relationship between God and the human bodies which many of us identify ourselves with as the actual being. You are god in your own body. If you wish to communicate with God, be your own intermediary, for rest assured that were God to come crashing down into your sphere of operation in answer to one of your prayers, dust would not even remain of the body which is yours, yet the soul which had been at the helm of that life would remain ... *embarrassed maybe,* to give it a human emotion, at having interfered with God's attention for the furtherment of one selfish little life.

There is no purpose in claiming that you are any way other than the way that you are. Be *you* to the best of your ability, and aspire onward and ever upward. There is no finer thing in existence, *to be,* other than you, so you may as well concentrate your efforts on *that* unique being. If your interest exists in things cosmic, let me describe How To Create A Solar System ...

How To Create A Solar System

The reality of such possibility is of secondary importance to the amount of inspiration potential existing in the exploration of capacity inherently available within each and every one of us human beings right now.

It is however, my understanding that when we reach a certain spiritual stability, for most of us aeons ahead of present time, the creation of a solar system will be but one option available to our evolutionary wave. Those readers who have assimilated material from my earlier works, and others tuned to a similar wavelength, will follow that if we are currently able to physically manifest that which we mentally desire, it follows that as our skills and understanding of karma progress, so too will our abilities become more powerful, in ratio to our ethical poise of course.

You may wish at this moment in time, for the purpose of example, to create a globe in your own mental universe, and set it spinning off into an orbit, which will see it disappear correspondingly as does your attention on it dwindle. Ponder the capacity and strength of a planetary logos, with pure focus on the globe for which full responsibility must be undertaken at all time if that spinning ball is not to disintegrate and go the way all will eventually, but preferably in a controlled fashion.

There will be at least two types of reader perusing these words I write; one type will be hanging on every word, searching out each significance in an effort to devour all esoteric understanding from the flavour I am here creating, and there is another type who will patiently read on in the hope of material a little more tangible following as soon as is possible. Many other viewpoints will of course also exist on these words ... rubbish, highfalutin nonsense, inspirational, claptrap, far out verbiage, exciting, useful and thought provoking are just some inevitable descriptions.

Let me ask you this ... if the creation of a solar system is not possible for the humble human being at some time in a more glorious future, then what does evolution hold in store for our planetary race? Follow evolution from that moment many years ago when an animal body was first indwelt by a soul, representative of spirit; see the change that has shown itself as human purpose, to inject love, charity and understanding into an otherwise jungle mentality. We are winning. News to some I know, but a fact nevertheless.

As animals have become domesticated over the millennia, they have lived in ever closer proximity to our charitable and altruistic viewpoints, and such association is now making inroads into the genetic make up of our closest friends from the third kingdom, most especially it seems, dogs and cats.

We associate with elements from the fifth kingdom which some people call heaven, or the spiritual universe, and quite naturally find ourselves gradually imbibing the rarer inspiration available from therein, and as is happening to dogs and cats through their association with us, so too are we enjoying new potential through nirvanain *(a self made word meaning a pertinence to nirvana)* contact.

In my third book Empowerment, I quoted Yogi Ramacharaka as follows ...

> When the soul sees itself as a Center surrounded by its circumference - when the Sun knows that it is a

Sun, surrounded by its whirling planets - then is it ready for the Wisdom and Power of the Masters.

You are the sun mentioned in this quote, and in Empowerment, we used a cute illustration showing body parts such as the heart and liver, orbiting the indwelling spirit which is depicted by a little sunman.

The universal law of correspondence, ever the great inspiration and hope for the future of humanity, tells us, according to Hermetic philosophy, *as above so below; as below so above.* It therefore follows that it is merely a matter of time before we begin to emulate those great spiritual entities, which currently find themselves locked in a mental focus enabling a solar system to physically manifest for billions of years, as a part of our progress onward and upward ever!

Why not?

The solar logos manifesting the great nuclear ball of fire which enables human life as we know it to evolve, has its planetary logoi manifesting their globes and orbiting them around their central spiritual sun which is the solar logos. In turn I feel sure that this solar logos is playing some lesser part in a greater hierarchical strategy beyond our present comprehension.

All that is within your current sphere of influence comprises your solar system. If you destabilise it, spare a thought for the consequences emanating on ripples as far as your predominance penetrates. If you strengthen it, enjoy the stability readily viewed physically in the economies of many successful western democracies.

The answer to the title of this chapter in YOU AND ME MAKE THREE, is that you are already creating a solar system, and these words are merely designed to propel you into an assessment of how well you are creating this part microcosm part macrocosm. Any cosmos is merely a well ordered system of ideas. The Greek word kosmos is the etymon for our word cosmos, and means order, ornament or world. It seems that we humans thrive on order and are repelled by chaos. Our evolutionary track record can be readily seen ...

> What you are is what you have been
> Contemplating privately
> Secret thoughts come straight to view
> As your surroundings mirror you
> The world is merely what goes on
> Inside your own cerebrum

... is how I described this phenomenon poetically in my second book BEFORE THE BEGINNING IS A

THOUGHT. I know that I have quoted the poem many times before, but it is through constant repetition of positivity that many of us are helped to create a critical mass which enables us to penetrate the miasma often obscuring our next step along the way.

Good luck with the creation of your solar system. If your cosmos and my cosmos make another cosmos not readily reducible into its constituent parts without the loss of some element or another, who will take responsibility for that cosmos? You and me, is the answer. Responsibility is never ending my friend, and it seems the more you take, the more you are expected to take. *Always give a job to a busy man,* states the aphorism, meaning that a person is busy because of personal abilities, one of which must be response-*ability*. Likewise it is sagacious to trust a person demonstrating responsibility, and this can often be seen manifesting as a well ordered life of creativity.

If you and me make three, and there are already existent zillions upon quadrillions of galaxies and solar systems, it soon becomes apparent that this incredible world in which we live should not ever be seen as finite, and we should in fact begin tapping into to the infinite which is there for us all to access ... as and when our well ordered ideas are ready for it!

Inno And The Angels

Angels angels everywhere, but never when you need one most! What do they do? Where do they come from? Do they have wings? Are they kind? Can they fly? Do they know God better than we do? Can you call on one in an emergency? Do they form a parallel evolution to that of humanity?

Questions questions everywhere, even when you need them least! 69% of Americans believe in angels, 25% do not, and 46% claim to have their own Guardian Angel, frequently exhibited as being in existence through the wearing of a lapel pin, whereas

21% do not. If the link between Guardian Angel and human is less powerful with the lapel pin not worn is not quite clear, but one feels that this may indeed be the case through lack of physical affirmation.

On the Internet, literally thousands upon thousands of articles are to be found, some apparently written by angels themselves, though these literate angels must learn to spell and present their work in more accurate and grammatical context if they are to be pursued by mainstream publishing houses; this is a sardonic outlook you may feel, but I work in the personal development industry where many claims exist without any care for readers, listeners or seminar goers, and every care for what piece of PR is going to make something stand out from the rest, and I remain comfortable with this outlook whenever nefarious claims pass my way. In this case, when we do make actual contact with angels, we will find ourselves in the *cry wolf* syndrome, and the added curve is that such claims as I have described with a degree of suspicion may just be true!

Inno and I discussed this latent phenomenon of the last few thousand years which we both call *angel fixation,* and it stated the following ...

"There is no need *to believe* in angels, for they exist regardless of such human fixation; it is wiser that a divine aspirant becomes sensitive to all potential, existences and phenomena through remaining open in heart and mind!"

Wise words from my friend! I questioned it further about *remaining open* however, regarding the potential for an infiltration of negativity to be possible, as is the intended influx of positivity.

"It is your state of mind which decides what will come your way when opening yourself up to progress. A clean heart is essential when the energy is inflowed, for the least speck of dust in that area will form in your life the ugly equivalent of an oyster's pearl. It is your heart which determines that which is good or bad, and not the incoming energy itself. Okay, there are oddballs floating about this galaxy who delight in causing trouble wherever they can lay their hats or wings, but it is wise to concern yourself with goodness, for it is only through concentrating your mental power onto *anything,* that *anything* is given power. Evil remains inert until motivated by human thought, which is just the attention it needs to do its dastardly deeds."

I knew that, but wanted to know if Innominate thought angels actually existed; not as a metaphor but as physical life …

"What you want to know is *my viewpoint* on angels, which has nothing itself to do with angels. If you wish to know about angels then become sensitive to angels ... but if your purpose for such knowledge is merely to write a few Internet articles for the purpose of self aggrandisement and further confusion into the lives of those daring to contemplate beyond the norm, then I advise you to watch football instead. Less harm will be done this way!"

Strong words from Innominate regarding not angels, but the answers to life per se. It seems that when Inno encounters anything it turns such chance to advantage, usually not obviously, rather, by looking behind the headlines, so to speak, and blending the blatant into the hidden and vice versa.

I know about such tactics for I do that exact same thing myself; but someone has to ask the questions. When asking questions, as I frequently do of life, and at physical meetings of the PAC, it seems to others that I must not know the answers, and this exactly is the case, for when posing questions, if you retain a fixed viewpoint regarding the answers, then it is pointless to have posed the question in the first place! Innominate knows this also.

Alien spacepeople, very light beings, ascended masters, *(although why never ascended mistresses I have yet to discover)* prophets, dreamers, guardian angels, common or garden angels, new age this, scio that and more often than not plenty of the other, can all be found cluttering the Internet and general highways and byways of life, as viewpoints of humans on an area of life as fascinating as it is unseen. Use such information as inspiration by all means, but be particular about anything that you take onboard as your own, for it may not be relevant for your particular process at a given time.

Inno has not ever knowingly encountered angels, but has taken as its own second hand knowledge the following ...

"Angels are an evolution separated from humanity in concept. Whereby humankind has self choice, angels do not. On the whole, each evolution is unaware of the other, although this barrier is becoming less rigid now than it has been since the fall of man. Biblical angels are more likely to have been messengers, and guardian angels conceptually arrived in medieval times with the notion that each individual is born with an accompanying guardian angel who stands by the right shoulder as a voice of conscience. A modern view is that angels often walk around as regular humans for the purpose of helping. This is likely often confused with the fact that divine beings, not always angels, did and do walk with us mere mortals as they always have and always will do. This is from where divinity has often been attributed to kings, queens, emperors, empresses and indeed anyone seen to be leading a large number of incarnate souls.

If your angels inhabit a universe of similar density to ours, and have wings, then it seems they will need to be 4 metres across to achieve lift off for an 80 kilogram body, which must also have massive pectoral muscles. It is possible that for the purpose of crossing over onto our line of evolution, an angel may take a transient body such as that of a crow or a eucalyptus tree."

If this information is useful to you then ponder it; if not then discard it and continue with the rest of this book. Inno and I understand. You must be passionate about honing an ability to differentiate between that which will improve your life and that which will hamper its progress. Getting bogged down with too much information can lead to decades of drowsiness. There are many reasons why a human being decides to improve life, but do you know what the single biggest impelling force is?

Read on ...

Causes Of Decision To Improve Personal Life

What is it that occurs in personal life which impels a mortal to instigate positive changes? In my years of studying the world of personal development that answer overwhelmingly has been some kind of disaster. After one evening of focalising a spontaneous discussion, a lady told me that for her it was a fire in the kitchen. Divorce, death, ill health and lack of money all play their part, and for the personal developers who are really business or job developers, it is often simply a question of accruing data for purposes of promotion and being seen to apparently be better than a rival, after being seen as lesser in some way. Another kind of personal disaster for the ego really.

I arrived on the path of self improvement after wondering one day if there was more to life than met the eye; there was no disaster there bar the one which I would have announced had I not discovered that there actually *is* more to life than meets the unaccustomed eye!

The inspiration for this title arrived with a letter from someone who had listened to one of my audio programmes. Before being given this programme by his mother, he told me of an experience he'd had, after confessing a life of scepticism and general non spiritual aspirations ... *I had the realisation that everything was connected to everything else, and not just a feeling, I could see it in my mind as clear as anything; I felt at one with the universe.*

The problem for most of us is in *the recognition* of our sensations and intuitions. All around exists evidence that this world we inhabit is as small as we think it. Living is three dimensional only for those who refuse to tune into the waves of inspiration hovering around each of us, inviting participation in other dimensions such as, the etheric world, the astral world, your inner world, the mental planes, the world of souls and perhaps even that place where spirit *just is*.

What I often wonder is why there need be any external stimulation for human beings to instigate self improvement of what essentially is inherently known to be, and that is, human potential. Yet, some are content to ride on the backs of others who must work harder for those that must work lesser. I have no gripe about this fact of life and know it to be a contributing factor to the variety which makes human existence so *almost* imponderable at times.

Karma is the great leveller, but knowledge of this fact only serves to impel many into a stressful *life of service* to save their own skins, and this is such a big misunderstanding of responsibility. There is only one legitimate reason for personal development to be instigated ...

You should improve yourself because you can!

There is no stress in that statement, only an observation of actuality, that nothing stays the same in the knowable universe; things get better or become worse. I am merely inviting all with whom I come into contact, to choose the former lest the latter gets a grip and sends you down the slippery slope to ruin!

The problem of self improvement is that word *self*. If individual growth does not have positive implications for the complete sphere of personal influence, then something is wrong. Ego trips ensue and the personal development industry gets a bad name, with the wayward ego as the guilty party.

You have to disassociate personal growth from the material world in the first instance, and discover yourself; who, what and where you really are. Once you are in possession of those facts, you will be in a better position to know what course of action is best for the particular type of person you are. It could be that fabulous wealth is an important part of your life cycle this time round, just as it could be *you* that needs the unfortunate experience of poverty. Whatever it is, you should do it well if you are to live up to the expectations of the human potential concept.

This is exactly what personal development is about ... whoever, whatever and wherever you are, *be yourself* and live to your fullest potential, *and not someone else's fullest potential!* Now, we have talked about the various impelling reasons for entering the world of self improvement, but the fact of the matter is, that you will improve with evolution almost regardless of the individual effort which you place at the door of growth. All personal development seeks to accomplish is a mirroring of the spiritual world of initiation. An initiation is only the quickening of evolution for an individual, or perhaps even a whole race or planetary civilisation. Once any initiation is undertaken, the result is further responsibilities. This is a paradox many find difficult to comprehend, we are so instilled with the fact that at the end of any effort is some kind of everlasting rest, but in actual fact the more effort you give over to development, the more will be required of you. The more responsibility you earn the "more extra" you will be expected to carry.

So if your brand of self improvement does not

show signs of wearing you out, beware, for it may not be happening! Many a plateaux will be apparent to you on your progress forward and ever upward, on which you may rest and gather your strength, but I cannot quote to you one example of anyone, once cognisant of human potential, who has sat back and said, *that's enough for this lifetime.* It is just not possible to do this, because the questions burn into your mind until you must attend the fires ... you can either get better or get worse, but again, I do not know of any examples illustrating successful human inertia. Look into the skies and show me anything that is still and not going one way or another. Not even the crusty old moon is inert; it performs a service to us every single night by deflecting the sun's energy onto our planet, and accomplishes this whilst, as many believe, it is dying!

There should be no need whatsoever for any external cause to impel a person into developing human potential; we must just do it because we can!

Innominate Tackles The Cynics

Unlike Hoover and Xerox, Univac has not lasted as an English language *verb taken from a noun,* but nevertheless Univac was the first computer introduced to us during the American presidential election of 1952, and as have most of its successors, it proved itself accurate. In those days however, we were unsure how far to trust this new technology, and in the case of that mentioned election, the computer's statistics were altered at the last minute to harmonise more closely with tried and tested human predications, which in this case were wrong, the computer having been right all the while.

To trust or not to trust is ever the question!

Computers were known as Univacs for a while afterwards, but the term did not become verb-*ised* because *things they were a changing* so fast! They are still, and ever faster it seems! Where is the Univac now? We hear in computer circles about IBM, Microsoft and even the AppleMac, but not the Univac.

What comes first, trusting of others, or trusting of you by others?

When Innominate dipped into the business world,

it began selling products to new age shops, along with mainstream retail outlets. Inno identified with the sentiments boasted as modus operandi by these new age shops and trusted that their actions would match their beautiful words. This was not to be however, and the trust was abused as many shops reneged on agreed payments even when all of the purchased products had been sold.

Innominate asked what should be done and I suggested that such shops should no longer be serviced. "Is this another way of not trusting others?" I was further questioned. "No," I answered, "trust is a two way energy; if it is breached in either direction, trust no longer exists."

*Your*trust + *another*trust = TRUST

The trust in capital letters is the gestalt which cannot be broken down into its constituent parts without the remaining of that magical ingredient, illustration of which this book is all about! When trust is broken, you must retreat, reconsider, *and rejoice if not a lot has been lost!* If the trust is to be repaired, for *repair* is what it is when the original has at any time been abused, the breaker of that trust must cognite on what has occurred, make moves to contact you and instigate the repair.

I hear of many other ways to handle these situations of trust breaking, such as ... *if you really care you will ignore any breach of your trust and keep seeking the relationship you sought before the trust was broken.* Well, you can try, but most times I have found that this does not work. To be crude about it, there are takers and givers; if you fall into either of these categories solely, then this book is not really for you. I have written it for the purpose of inspiring balanced people, or at least those who have balance as an aspiration and can see it nearby.

Relationships, whereby one party is a taker and the other a giver, are aberrated and can almost be related to sadomasochistic affairs, where one is a

sadist and the other a masochist! These books and audio programmes which I research, prepare, write and record, are actually designed for those of us who are already able. They are not therapy oriented; readers and listeners will already be above any need for therapy, or at least have transcended any previous need for therapy of any description, before arriving at the concept of these programmes in agreement that they are helpful. It sounds harsh but this is the way it is!

Balanced relationships, well, they just kind of balance themselves! If you seek to trust someone who is not balanced, then place your hand in the mouth of the tiger by all means, but do not expect the tiger to not see your hand as a meal.

So, I write for the able, and therefore my description of the *trust gestalt* is also for the able. The *win for all* scenarios which I describe as desirable in all deals and business of any description, are based on the fact that you will be exchanging with a balanced counterpart. When this is not the case then brace yourself for trouble, if those with whom you wish to deal are beneath a certain tone level of life. What is a tone level of life? It is a vibration. If you have good vibes and bad vibes, it is wise to deal with those above the midway point separating good from bad.

We can return for the *trust renegades* after the able have realised a greater proportion of human potential than that so far achieved. For the time being leave the *trust renegades* to deal with their counterparts; sooner rather than later it will be realised that no worthwhile future exists for those incapable of trust and trustworthiness.

If you wish to live life as does a wildebeest at the waterhole, forever looking behind itself checking that the tiger does not have sight of it, then double cross a few colleagues and sit back as life shows you how it works.

Innominate once again trades with new age shops; a passage of time elapsed, and with it came another rule … *it is wise to retain a flexible approach if you are to succeed in all that you contemplate and act upon.* The computer on which these words were written was just about the most powerful machine available at the time. I viewed the words on a 21 inch high resolution good refresh rate monitor driven by a 4 megabyte video card. The computer itself is a Pentium pro 200 kilohertz, 32 megabyte Ram, 16 bit sound card with 44.1 kilohertz digital recording software, 2 gigabyte SCSI hard drive, 8 times speed SCSI CD ROM *beast of a machine!*

By the time you read these words the preceding

specification may be laughable. That is also what happens when a viewpoint is retained beyond its sell by date ...

Be flexible. Be strong. Have integrity. Be courageous. Develop thought power. Be charitable. Be love ... and above all **be yourself** ... otherwise you could end up like the Univac.

And that is not a threat ... its a joke!

The Odessa Phial
Sasha Flies To London

With seventy years of communist propaganda tucked neatly under his belt, Sasha thought he would have a stab at capitalism. The Berlin Wall had fallen and the Russian satellites had soon followed by withdrawing their previously enforced economic and social allegiance to the monstrous state grouping which had been known as the Union of Soviet Socialist Republics.

Of course the amount of propaganda tucked neatly under Sasha's belt was in no way indicative of his corporeal age; no, it just meant the Soviet way had been so all embracing that the sum total of all indoctrination seemed to be involuntarily inculcated into any soul which brushed within its sphere of influence. Sasha had been within this mentioned sphere of influence for only thirty nine years, but five of those years were spent in the army, and so counted as ten.

Now if this writing seems critical, or borders on the facetious, then it is not accomplishing the author's intention, which is to shed light on a most awkward human affliction; the one which leads us to believe that we are doing something, which in living fact is very different from that action in which execution we are actually involved. We could make up a name for this affliction and perhaps gain credence in the world of psychology; as Sasha speaks Russian we can give it that old Soviet feel just to put the frighteners on anyone who feels compelled to practice this most unworthy of human conditions: WILEISKY ... *the act of thinking you are doing something, whilst in actual fact accomplishing something else.*

Sasha flew to London and described himself as a phial seeking to contain the liquid energy required to empower his workforce. He had a pained expression on his face whenever I spoke of something outside his then current area of interest ... our meeting began without a formal dawning; it just kind of moved from chat to talk to viewpoint exchange, to discussion to statements of intent, back to chat before good-byes.

He was a psychologically oriented individual; all of his motives, conclusions and actions required mental blessing from his thought processes, and whenever I veered from this comfort zone, that old pained expression returned to his face. Sasha, short for Alexander, *why I do not know,* was a Ukrainian, born and raised in the Black Sea resort of Odessa, famous for its spars and visible sun, whilst most other parts of the old Soviet empire were in bleak twilight. With American backing, he had made and lost a million American dollars within a year of perestroika and glasnost finding their ways into western vocabularies, and this qualified him for the altitude of mentor, within the realms of his peers back in Odessa. He was now quite safety conscious with respect to the art of *maintaining* wealth, and this resulted in a somewhat dour outlook on anything which did not stink of big profits.

Sasha owned most of my books, and audio cassette tape programmes which were his particular favourite medium for the dissemination of personal development material. We spoke of American ways, and he described the American outlook on self help as a conveyor belt approach … *hatch a formula and shove the people through a system derived from that formula, resulting in maximum financial rewards for the inventors of that formula ...* Sasha's idea, my definition!

He revelled in the ancientness of Eastern European traditions which he condescendingly felt these new fangled Americans could not possibly understand, and so to London. We met in the new PeRFECT WORDS and MUSIC INTERNATIONAL LTD offices located close to Gatwick airport. From the staggering losses he suffered only a few years earlier, Sasha had grown with a company which now employed more than 100 people. As I have said, he was highly motivated by money, but he voiced his main concern from a humanitarian viewpoint, by asking for my help in showing his workforce just what was available to them, using my personal development material, along with any other theory which would help them.

I asked why he really wanted to help them, and Sasha spoke of a desire to make his good fortune in contacting this exploratory area of human potential, available to his people. We spoke of the possibility for workshops, seminars, talks and manuals; at one point I was to stay at the swish London Sky Hotel after being flown to Odessa, all expenses paid with a good fee, just to be available for these most fortunate of employees.

I wondered!

He talked about distributing thousands of copies of the recently published into Russian version of YOU CAN ALWAYS GET WHAT YOU WANT.

I wished!

We discussed translations for all of my work.

I hoped!

He then talked again about his employees and asked for my help.

I knew!

"I will be pleased to help your workers Sasha," I said, "but it is on the condition that it is they I help, and only indirectly you and your company, often in ways which will not be apparent at the time"

"How can that be Phil?" he asked, "if you show these people what is available to them, they will work harder; how can I lose?"

"That is the American way is it not?" I ventured, "my outlook on self help has nothing whatsoever to connect it with business, and it could be that after I have worked with your people, half of them will leave their jobs after realising that working for you is not how they wish to spend their life on this earth. The other half may not do as they are told which I am sure is not part of your wish, and this will leave me in the precarious position of seeming to drain your company of funds whilst scaring the workforce into the hands of your competitors. The fact that any employee who leaves, will in actual fact be a blessing in disguise if that person was not living an inspired story through working for you, will be one of those indirect benefits which I doubt you will realise at the time"

That old pained expression returned to Sasha's face as I am sure he wondered why on earth he was sitting there in front of me. I saw my fee disappear and reminisced about the last time such a situation had reared its head. A network marketing company had invited my to deliver the keynote speech at their annual gathering. I was asked to motivate and ready them for the rest of the evening, which would be spent telling them all about the potential for individual wealth within that company, all the while closely *(and cynically)* connecting it with personal development. I didn't do it then and I wouldn't ever!

"What long term impact will that type of speech have on the lives of your audience?" I asked, before explaining that perhaps it would be better for us to prepare an evening of maximum benefit for all.

"I just want them *whooping* in the aisles," was the last description of what was required of me before I declined the invitation, thus rendering the fee a potential of the past.

Sasha's new company was built around a fact that for the first few years of its existence, it would not attract any government taxes, and in fact would also be able to import free of duties, any items it deemed relevant for the advancement of the new capitalist Ukrainian society. This led the company into utilising its duty free status for the gain of other companies not entitled to such benefit, with a resultant splitting of further profits at the expense of the Ukrainian people. As Sasha now operated in the realms of consumer durables, he hatched a plan for the publishing of a WHICH type magazine, the purpose being to elicit compulsory rave reviews for all the products he represented in the Ukraine.

"A person cannot do right in one department, whilst attempting to do wrong in another," were Gandhi's words which continuously flashed across my mental field of vision ... unfashionable with those who want a quick fix from the realms of human potential, most especially wileiskies!

This phial called Sasha, who sought to contain the liquid energy required to empower his workforce, was no different to any manager who wants to extract the last drop of energy from the workers. In fact this phial was more detrimental than most regular managers because he dressed up his intentions in fancy words, fashionable phrases, a modicum of psycho-babble and a disguise of personal development.

This was such a shame ... the idea of Odessa had been inviting!

Inno's Physical Challenge

We have received so many words from both Innominate and myself during this book, that my own thoughts were turned to the more physical aspects of life. It is so easy for me to talk, write and create in mental matter, all that contents my heart, but it seems plain that this world is dense, solid and at times ostensibly immovable. In the spirit of the 1917 Russian, communist revolution, I asked Inno whether or not the workers were more important than the aristocracy, intelligentsia, or in fact any other strata of society seemingly above them; it answered ...

"Why must we perceive relative importances as an operating mechanism for healthy living on Planet Earth? This globe on which we have our lives, is a body comprised of cells. We are those cells; spleen cells within the human body are different to the teeth cells and one cell finds it difficult to live without the other, though in the case of this example, not impossible. The spleen as an abdominal organ, concerns itself with the production and removal of blood cells and forms part of the immune system. The teeth are utilised for the mastication of food, without which the spleen would be unnecessary as death ensues within weeks of food deprivation.

So, this planet is also comprised of cells with varying roles. **All is spirit;** do not forget this tenet, for it describes the divinity of densest matter and saint alike. Saints know this, but densest matter finds it quite a difficult concept to comprehend. As this world is run by human beings metaphorically falling upper midway between saint and stone, we assign individuals a class to which they belong, and call those perceived as beneath us, *lesser,* and those perceived to be above us, *greater.*

This is idiocy at its most human my friend! The greater needs the lesser in exact ratio to the needs of the lesser for the greater. Neither is quite aware of this until disaster strikes shoving complacent individuals out of a comfort zone and into enforced fresh thoughts. Cognitions appear, but are frequently ignored as the comfort zone is once again sought.

It's a funny old world isn't it?"

I asked Innominate if it is important to be capable of performing physical tasks which you are asking others to perform for you by proxy.

"Why should it be? If you spend a year writing, recording and promoting a rock music album which the manual worker is less able to do, yet is entertained by your offering, why is it that both feel a need to be capable of performing the other's task. In short, the answer is no!

If you wish to pursue this question of physical challenges, then let me illustrate a potentially helpful scenario which will cease your questioning of me along this line.

If there has to be a hierarchy then it is a spiritual hierarchy, but this is not comprised of beings judging humanity as we each seem to humanly judge each other, although this is the typical human viewpoint of all perceived as being above humanity. Each of us will eventually take our seats in this great council, which paradoxically is unable to alter the free choice and will of humanity, even when disaster is sensed."

"What is the purpose of such a council then?" I interjected with trepidation and a sense of loneliness.

"To inspire, guide, hint and give clues; not quite like the county councils or state legislatures that you likely have in your mind as a model for my description. Quite unlike parliaments, congresses and senates, the spiritual hierarchy is a group of evolved beings, each taking responsibility for a specialised aspect of existence. Parliaments, congresses and senates are merely the lower physical harmonics of such spiritual governing bodies, much as the telephone is a lower harmonic of our innate ability for telepathy.

The great beings of whom we here speak, are beyond the human emotion of judgement, and seek only to help humanity as a service. You and I will one day in the future take up our seats in the great council chamber and continue this service, thus allowing the present incumbents to move onwards and ever upwards.

This we call evolution.

The inspiration we seek for our efforts on earth, emanates from such places as this great council chamber, along with many other locations, and beings from other spiritual departments. We must here mention that inspiration is also available from each personal soul, the ease of access for which is dependent on the amount of soul contact an individual has achieved at any one point of that group of lifetimes for which the soul has overseen ... not in a linear line, as we insist upon visualising, but as an holistic experience of many lifetimes consisting of incarnations and deaths.

To help with our visualisation of the holistic soul experience, let us consider the following ... all soul cycles may be considered as consisting of ...

birth ... living ... death

... birth from the soul perspective, you may find helpful to ponder as physical death, living you may consider as the between physical lives experience, and death visualise as physical birth, all the while remembering that nothing stops, and all is in a continuous stage of evolution, whether in a degenerative stage or a creative portion.

creation ... transformation ... destruction

This cycle of action describes all aspects of existence that we are able to ponder, and must note that there is no negativity attached to the *destruction* portion of the cycle. Destruction can be a most creative aspect of life and is ever necessary for the furtherance of life as a whole ... *we are the cells of this whole.*

You ask if we should be willing to engage in the manual work that we ask others to perform for us, and my answer is, that to the degree one is capable of inspiring such work, a contribution to its actual execution has been made! It is amazing what can be pondered through the simple act of considering physical challenge."

I understood all that Innominate communicated to me, but could not resist one last question, not that I was totally non cognisant of the answer, but in the hope of putting myself and it together to make a new ingredient for the pot. I asked …

"Is thought as physical as stone?"

"Yes; to the degree that it is *thought* on which you are focused, then it is as physical, although rarer, as the stone with which you build your lesser council chambers."

I noted the tongue in cheek remark, as did Innominate, with a passing smile. It continued …

"All is spirit, remember? Thought is just as physical as any aspect of our tangible world. The stuff from which we create thought is rarer, lighter and more malleable; it therefore follows that working in mental matter is so much quicker than when working in manual labour. You are able to create a complete solar system in thought stuff and that solar system is an actuality. To hold it in place for millennia would

take mental effort beyond our present capacities however, let alone to plan other life evolving inside of it. With additional power brought about through service of humanity, study and meditation, we will be able to place enough focus and attention upon our creations for others to call it matter. For the time being we utilise goals and plans to materialise objects which inevitably end up being formed with the help of human touch. In the not too distant future, that human touch too will be mental."

I thanked Inno for the time and consideration it had shown me. Yet again, a combination of myself and it, had formed a third force ever more potent than either of us singly. This made me feel good! I wondered what 1+1 would equal were those two digits to represent the spiritual hierarchy and us aspiring classes, in a knowing pursuit of synergy.

I think we should give it a try!

MANUAL

Wouldn't it be nice if there was a little red book in which lay revealed for all to read, the answers to life's questions? Chairman Mao told the population of China that he'd written one and it became one of the most widely distributed books ever; mind you it was free and compulsory to the one billion or so mainland Chinese. In fact every dogmatic faith or political system seems to produce such a book and all adherents appear magically to cognite that their book or strategy is the only answer to any mystery which may have previously surrounded their lives.

The Bible is an obvious example, but there are many lesser known tomes serving the fixations of adherents all over the world. The Scientologists have Dianetics The Modern Science of Mental Health, which, according to the son of its author, was written off the top of L Ron Hubbard's head in a few days. In Hubbard's early days of writing science fiction, I read that when short on cash, he announced to fellow writers, Asimov amongst them I believe, that the quickest way to make money was to start a religion, which he then did. Earlier in this book you will have read about an actor I know who decided to be a psychiatrist; in this act he was successful and actually helped people.

What is it that makes the Moonies Moonies? Why do kids leave the local comprehensive school, shave their heads, join the Krishna Temple and chant whilst running down Oxford Street in London clinking cymbals? How do people get themselves into a state which compels them to kill for Islam. How? Why? What? When?

If you are reading this book then you must have transcended the urges I am here describing, but this does not detach you from the effect they still have on society regardless of your direct participation. PHIL MURRAY PERSONAL DEVELOPMENT states that any mentor who leaves you with a feeling of dependency, is not performing the task of teaching correctly. The age in which we find ourselves incarnate, has as its dominant energy that of Aquarius. Now this has little relating it to fairground fortune tellers or your stars in a local newspaper; any truth becomes weakened into a myriad of dilutions almost in ratio to the amount of differing types of human being alive at any one time. The pure Aquarian energy pouring into our sphere of awareness is as factual as was the Piscean energy which became dominant at the same time as that great being known as Jesus The Christ arrived 2,000 years ago.

There are crossover periods of around 500 years, as one energy supplants another, and we find ourselves living at a time when this most recent changeover is almost complete, and the dominant astrological energy is becoming very strong ... with this energy has arrived new opportunities related to the peculiar qualities inherent within the astrological age in which we live.

If I had written 2,000 years ago, the words I have just previously stated ... *any mentor who leaves you with a feeling of dependency, is not performing the task of teaching correctly* ... it would have been incorrect. That astrological age had as an integral part of it the urges of devotion, dependency and belonging, usually to a monolithic type organisation of dogmatic religious interpretation devoted to some great seer or other.

We are now at a stage of development where all answers to everything can be found within. Books, teachers and lectures are useful only as stimulation and inspiration, but the paradox is that the most useful amongst us *will* form groups to enable a greater understanding of the new wisdom which is all around us in this newly mental oriented world of ours. In line with the title of this book ... YOU AND ME MAKE THREE ... 1+1=3 ... *your wisdom plus the wisdom of another produces wisdom not belonging to either one individual contributor,* I urge you to find others also sensitive to human potential and form groups. Unlike the monolithic organisations redolent of the Piscean age now passed, people will attach themselves to groups only through an understanding of the potential contained within such a group, and the service to humanity such a group can offer.

I remember watching an interview with Keith Richards of Rolling Stones fame; he was asked how he wrote songs like Honky Tonk Woman, Brown Sugar and Angie … his answer was remarkable in that it was a total acknowledgement of all about which I here write. He said that he had not ever really written a song in his life … *I just tune in to whatever is hanging around, it usually makes a good song but I haven't got a clue where it comes from.*

Whether it is a song, book, lecture, poem, or in fact any piece of information in which you have interest, I urge you to cease thinking about it and begin inspiring. I have to be careful when making these urges, because they can be misinterpreted as irresponsible. I can clarify this by explaining that the human mind is not just capable of thinking everyday type thoughts … if you quieten such activity it enables human contact with the infinite body of everything. Most people are too busy thinking their clever, exclusive little contemplations about themselves, to access *the great all* for infinite potential.

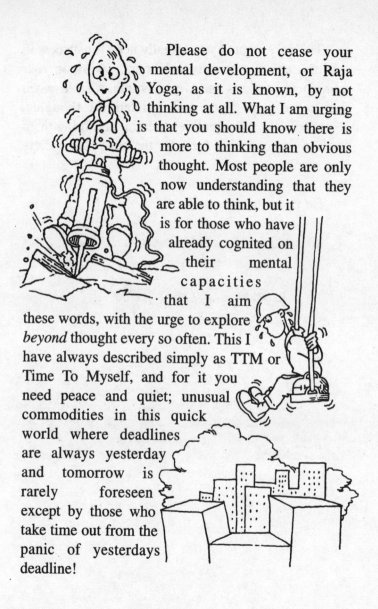

Please do not cease your mental development, or Raja Yoga, as it is known, by not thinking at all. What I am urging is that you should know there is more to thinking than obvious thought. Most people are only now understanding that they are able to think, but it is for those who have already cognited on their mental capacities that I aim these words, with the urge to explore *beyond* thought every so often. This I have always described simply as TTM or Time To Myself, and for it you need peace and quiet; unusual commodities in this quick world where deadlines are always yesterday and tomorrow is rarely foreseen except by those who take time out from the panic of yesterdays deadline!

The only manual you actually need for success in this new age of Aquarius, is labour ... work on your own focus towards the world within, visible when you close your eyes and quieten all thoughts. Discover your own qualities therein, and bring them forth in demonstrable form for the benefit of society as a whole.

Be your own manual!

INNOMINATE WAGES A HOLY WAR
Battleground Earth

Love and peace are not related to those sad human conditions of being walked all over and trodden upon. Love and peace are ever stronger than their counterparts of fear and turmoil; those of us exhibiting the described conditions as true soul characteristics, mistakenly referred to frequently in the context of personality oriented emotions erroneously called love and peace, when really the intended meaning is irrational, unfettered devotion and attachment mixed with indolent placidity, are the strength of the planet.

> ***Turning the other cheek*, means not reacting to the antagonistic emanations of other lower minds needlessly.**

There has never been planetary peace at any moment during the twentieth century. Wars between nations, skirmishes, terrorism and covert hostilities have been constant, and dwarfed only in our consciousness by the major world war which came to be known as a duality and consequently named using its sections, 1 and 2. I feel this state of regionalised turmoil will change by the early twenty first century, but do not hold your breath until the first twenty five years of it have passed.

I was eager to know if Innominate experienced peace and asked exactly that. The answer came swiftly and helpfully, as ever ...

"I know little about the planetary disagreements you have mentioned, but can honestly tell you that despite my wisdom, and at the risk of self depreciating in your estimations of me, I have never been at peace this lifetime."

This took me a little by surprise. If something or one, the spiritual calibre of Innominate, was unable to experience peace within its own life, then what chance I of consummating my undoubted aspiration for the concept of inner calm. Inno continued its explanation with acknowledgement of my questioning expression ...

"You feel that because of some spiritual endowment you have afforded me, inner peace should accompany it. That is what you think and must never be confused with actuality; remember, the mind is the map and not the territory itself. Inside of me is a jihad and I have issued a fatwa that islam must prevail."

So many Arabic words all of a sudden left me cold. It was the Islamic overtones of fanaticism which blocked the way for my understanding of that which Innominate sought to communicate. Inno knew this and continued …

"The jihad of which I speak, is a holy war against the unbeliever which is my lower self, my lower mind and my animal instincts. The fatwa which I have issued is my own authoritative ruling on a religious matter, which for me is the fact that I insist my higher self, higher mind and spiritual instincts prevail at all times, which they do not at present, but islam will be. This islam of which I speak is *submission to god,* and submit to god I will, for god is this higher self from which I seek to live out my lives with increasing power and effect! *Islam* comes from the word *aslama,* which means resign oneself, and this is what my lower self is in turmoil over, resigning itself to me the aspiring higher self"

I understood.

"When will this war be over," I asked, risking, or rather inviting further admonishment regarding my lack of knowledge in this department ...

"The battleground is earth my friend; whenever rare spirit, in this case taking the form of a mediator we call the soul, is brought into contact with denser spirit, or matter, holy war will result. The crusades of the middle ages were merely exoteric frustrations of what could not at that time be realistically accomplished within. The opposition to the plan of god was deemed therefore to be external, and useless wars were fought for no good reason. The real opposition to god is within, and can be cleansed through affirmation, along with *service of humanity, charity and goodwill;* the latter three have already been frequently referred to; no apologies offered however, for such apologies would be less purposeful than the frequent references to truth, however superficially boring."

"Is the lack of inner peace you describe as your present life, a greater peace than the apparent peace of those not yet aware of such conflict?" I asked this question which had been nudging me to vocalise it since Inno mentioned the crusades ...

"Lesser, greater, what does it matter. We are each partaking of different incarnate processes, which all inevitably lead to the same place. Consequently, we are experiencing varied stages of development, and what one person feels, another is either immune to, or has not yet reached a sensitivity whereby that feeling can be felt. My current state of peace, despite the turmoil and negative sounding scenario which you may have interpreted my words as describing, is in fact incredibly satisfying, for the battleground that I have mentioned is my particular process for this specific state of awareness which I currently enjoy. If I were not able to do battle, then I would be unhappy; a state of suppression would prevail and this is indeed the nastiest human condition on which we both inflict between humans, but more relevantly for this context, inflict upon ourselves."

"During the crusades," I began, "opposing groups always felt that God was on their particular side. Does it ever occur to you that your lower self may feel this patriotism too?"

"Not at all; the lower self seeks only to survive as a highly evolved animal, with no disrespect intended to the animal kingdom; actually and incidentally service of this animal kingdom is the purpose of humanity as a whole, along with service of the plant and mineral kingdoms. *We consistently plunder that which we should be serving!* How human! Not for much longer, I feel. I was reading the Alice Bailey book called ESOTERIC PSYCHOLOGY I yesterday, and noted some words which describe better than I have been able to so far, the state of a human life were it to be soulless ...

> (... man's body nature or personality is a distinct organism, separable from him as a soul) ...

It is the soul which seeks all things higher at present, and perhaps in a few more million years time, the soulless body, maybe evolving within the animal kingdom under a group soul, will also seek communion with a growing god within.

Mayhap ... perchance ... maybe ... perhaps!"

The most explosive equation in history took on new dimensions and significances, as I once again began to ponder 1+1=3 ... where 1 is the lower self and the other 1 is the higher self ... what must 3 signify? Communion with God, victory, service or just plain regularly mentioned evolution, where everything is urged to move from low to high ... onwards and upwards ever.

Well, no incarnate human quite knows the answer to this at present, but it is in pondering of the question that a critical mass will be created, which inevitably must become so strong that a breakthrough occurs. That breakthrough will be the answer, which itself will quickly become insignificant as the next answer within this equation is sought.

Where will it all end?

INNER POWER

How successful are you at closing your eyes and contemplating your awareness *as* another universe or dimension? Many people speak about their inner world, but fewer actually have a good understanding of it. An increasingly positive acquaintance with the invisible, (for the time being) is however, of paramount importance for all but the flimsiest of personal development.

Any sort of development that you can accomplish without accessing your inner world is of the external variety, and akin to home decoration, getting a better job, copying someone who is already good at an aspect of life in which you desire to become more accomplished, buying a big, fast car, a new suit, or even of the inverted variety where people become deliberately poor, scruffy and inept in all they do.

Inner power is becoming adept in all that you touch, and if you wish, all the lesser and exoteric appropriations necessary for a comfortable human existence can also be yours; to have it the other way round which is the norm, sees people becoming increasingly unhappy the better they do. Witness the amount of famous actors, or musicians, who become aimless in their private lives whilst exhibiting all the apparencies of happiness in their public equivalent.

People are usually too busy to contact the one part of life which can bring them the true happiness and power they seek through being busy in the first place.

When you think, it is in the mental universe, from which all more dense existence is thought, or created. Increasing numbers of humanity are becoming mentally oriented, as opposed to the more instinctive, *not intuitional,* living which had been the norm. This is evolution. Thinking is another type of busy-ness however, and not one from which I seek here to dissuade you, as it is through a greater acquaintance with your thinking mechanisms which should lead you ever closer to something far more powerful.

When you stop thinking, or quieten your mind, and begin to *just be,* which frighteningly enough for some, is the end product of all human type personal development, you will find yourself in the realms of para-humanity; not many of us are there yet, but all influence finding its way down into more dense forms of existence, will have either passed through this plane, or actually have been expired from it.

It is an area in which utilisation of the brain type consciousness is futile, and again, one must begin yet another round of personal development in this mental environment, through sensing what is expected *from* you as a service, and *for* you as a kind of human withdrawal of power. To use this access *purely* for personal gain is the equivalent of placing your hand inside a bomb as it is about to explode. Some become adept in this field of operation, but not all follow the right hand path of altruistic intent. The choice always remains with you, but firstly we have to get you in the area of power where that decision will be crucial.

No amount of ritual, chants, mantras, teacher following, book reading, lecture listening or god worshipping will get you there; you may find inspiration which can add impetus to the desire for soul contact, but the final thrust awaits only your command. Just as you practice things in the physical universe like running, swimming and gardening, or you study manuals in order to make your computer and its software, television or video run smoothly, so too must even more attention be given over to exploration of your inner power, although this will not necessarily involve you in devoting an inordinate amount of time to it. Attention and time are not necessarily synonymous!

All you have to do is do it! Just get down to the business of doing it! Define that word procrastination and then affirm it out of your vocabulary. Don't get stressful about doing it … just do it. I am stressing that word *do* because that is what humanity will find a challenge as it become increasingly mentally oriented. You have seen, or can imagine, a person on hallucinogenic drugs, or someone experiencing virtual reality with a computer headset … they become divorced from the physical and immersed in the mental. This too can happen when one makes successful contact with the upper realms, where inner power becomes apparent.

If you find being alone in quiet stillness with your eyes closed a little unconfrontable, then apply gradual graduation and do it bit by bit. Begin with one minute … you will wish to continue, for that is not long enough to satisfy human curiosity, but do not. Continue the following day with two minutes; the same phenomenon may occur, but again discontinue your indrawn attention after the prescribed duration. Day by day increase the amount of time you spend *inside,* and begin to note your particular orientation as you so do. When you are comfortable in meditation for twenty or so minutes, you will then know yourself how to continue and my words will cease to be helpful as senior to your own knowingness.

Inner power is a force of the universe. It doesn't belong to anyone in particular; it is a reservoir of mental stuff awaiting utilisation. This mental stuff is not good or bad, for the colour of it is what you assign when using it. Before you access this plane, let me tell you that it is almost irresistible not to try this power out for your own amusement or profit, and this again is natural and human; it is the intent which lies behind your actions and underlies all that you are, which I seek here to address. Keep your intentions clean and honourable, and even if they are not at present, like anything, with continuous affirmation and will, your intentions eventually fall into line with the divine purpose which is yours! A microcosm of that great macrocosmic energy from which we are all sparks.

Real inner power is the ability to make that spark which is you, shine so brightly that all will follow your example. All you need do to access this power ahead of the greater mass of humanity, is spend time and attention inside yourself.

Close your eyes, be still, do not think, be ... just be.

It is so simple that many think it cannot be

effective ... it isn't busy enough, or dense enough, or fun enough, or startling enough, or sensational enough, or ... enough? Enough!

Inner power equals calmness, knowingness, brightness and resolve; all of these qualities will also manifest physically. It is in your own personal interest and for the benefit of all humanity, that you access this inner power, for one day it will be the operational norm, just as now we shake hands and ask after the health of a friend. I write here only about being a pioneer, and portending by example what lies ahead for your fellow travellers.

Be light ... be love ... be power ... and before you can be these three qualities, you must just be!

INNOMINATE MEETS THE BANK MANAGER

Many years elapsed and the equivalent of countless physical centuries passed, before Inno and its mental universe felt a need and yearning to link up with the densest plane again. The mental universe in which Innominate felt most comfortable, was within easy reach of that great intuitional plane from where all of the finest ideas are inspired; one day, such an inspired idea was acted upon.

Innominate was moved to seek finance for a concept which seemed a success waiting to happen. In fact, lifetimes had passed by without even a cursory glance in the direction of self employment on earth; the time had come though, and Inno felt a duty to take this idea all the way ... well, part of the way, for the real motivation was purely illustrative.

It is tempting to ask why Innominate should need to seek finance in physical life from such a high state of awareness, and ask that you might. You may also answer that question for yourself as I shall not. It is not relevant to this story you see.

The nature of the idea was this ... get a loan from a bank to finance a scheme to canvass support from all of the banks, for the purpose of them feeding the starving human beings of the world with their surplus profits; the share holders would merely receive a slightly smaller dividend for one year. With clever schemes in place allowing these humans to quickly feed themselves forever, or thereabouts, trading could then begin with them for mutual profit and life support.

Irresistible … who could fail to be moved by such a plan … its a turn on!

Bank Manager
Good morning Mr Innominate, please take a seat.

Innominate
Thank you.

Bank Manager
What can I do for you?

Innominate
Its more what I can do for you actually (bank manager grimaces)

Bank Manager
That makes a change Mr Innominate, its usually the other way around! (with chuckle and eventual loud incongruous laugh)

Innominate
The nature of my idea is this … to get a loan from you to finance a scheme which will canvass support

from all of the banks, your rivals included, for the purpose of all of you feeding the starving human beings in the world with your surplus profits; your share holders will merely receive a slightly smaller dividend. With clever schemes in place allowing these humans to quickly feed themselves forever, or thereabouts, trading could then begin with them for mutual profit and life support. Simple!

Bank Manager (coughing, offers Innominate a cigar which is declined ... she lights one for herself)
Do you have any orders for your product yet?

Innominate
What product?

Bank Manager (checking her watch)
Oh yes ... I see what you mean. What about premises? Staff ... they don't come cheap you know Mr Innominate.

Innominate
I don't want them to come cheap.

Bank Manager
Oh yes ... I see what you mean.

Innominate
I thought that we could also eradicate female circumcision in the third world while we are on this project ... (bank manager crosses her legs) ... lots of needless suffering through lack of education, I'm sure you agree!

Bank Manager
Collateral?

Innominate
Bless you!

Bank Manager (blatantly lying)
Don't hesitate to call again if you have any more good ideas.

Innominate
I will!

If Innominate had wished to purchase an insurance agency, or perhaps an estate agency, it would have been so much easier, but two worlds collide when a creator is in the same space as one who merely lives life according to his, or in this case her, socialisation process.

I had a similar experience myself not so very long ago when we decided to once again explore the formation of a relationship with a bank ... we wished to launch ten *alternative medicine* audio programmes simultaneously, and for this we sought £20,000 as a loan from a bank. Similar questions were voiced, such as ... *Can you show me any orders? Who buys this sort of thing? Can you downgrade the quality to upgrade the profit? What is homeopathy? Where is your cash flow forecast? Are you prepared to place your house, insurance policies, children and genitals as collateral?*

In the mentioned case that bank tried to get around £800 from us in arrangement fees, quite apart from interest rates in keeping with far higher risks than was ours, bearing in mind the collateral called for, especially the two last bits! We told the bank that we would not ever do business with them whilst they remained so selfish and inflexible. Not that they cared much ... its more effective when 3,000 like minded souls get together and shout a mutual NO to them that they sit up and notice *things they are a changing*.

That reminds me of the phenomenal number of votes which the Green Party polled at a particular general election during the 1980's, indicating a sudden change of consciousness within the population of Great Britain towards environmental issues. The didn't win any seats in parliament, but certainly made the other old parties sit up and take note. They performed a service for us which continues its effect to this day.

It is not clever to allow the collision of two worlds, and my words merely serve to illustrate the point. If you want business with a bank then do it their way with as many fair benefits as you can muster going your way, but do not expect non creative people to suddenly get creative with you ... it may happen sometimes, but I here write about the norm and not the exception.

Innominate knew all of this and had the experience for the purpose of this work only. That is its nature.

If you want money then seek it, but if the reason for that search is purposeless or lacking integrity then note your weakness. Money is merely an exchange. Make a wish for it if you like, but know that it is a by-product of an otherwise unrelated service of humanity and its dependents. For that reason you would be better suited spending time in creation and action; the money will inflow in exact ratio to the standard of service you provide, in keeping with the mores and beliefs of those whom you serve.

The bank manager could not have said it better herself!

What Happens When You Make A Wish

Most people begin their own personal development engulfed in a trivial titillation. It is that phenomenon which states that *if you can think it you can have it;* this sets many en route to personal development of the disaster variety. Aspirants try thinking to get rich and end up *impatiently* chucking the books and tapes that told them to so do into the garbage, with the affirmation that never again will they try to improve themselves.

I rarely attempt to recapture the imagination of those disillusioned in this fashion. I am a guilty party however, being the original stimulus as an author and presenter, for many in this field of self help. Yet, the programme most likely to point people in the direction of possessions as the main aim of personal development, called You Can Always Get What You Want, states quite categorically that it is in the *service of others,* readers and listeners will be most likely to discover manifestations of whatever they desire to appear. A direct quote from that book is that **it is impossible to be a great giver and also unsuccessful in life,** but it seems many just tolerate the altruistic pointers in success programmes and head straight for the bits describing how to grab and run. Not everyone you understand, but I bet there is not one amongst us who has not thought about our own ends first and the needs of our neighbours second ... this is a natural part of evolution, seen as a microcosm of universal physics in every life. If you are using it as an excuse for an elongated portion of life in the grab department, beware; total lack of satisfaction eventually ensues and such *grab prolongation* can have devastating effects on any member of humanity past a certain point of evolutionary development ... in other words those to whom this work is targeted!

Even those who eventually become great philanthropic examples to the world have usually gone through a selfish phase, often around puberty, adolescence and young adulthood, where the world exists for their own service, rather than the other way around. Some of us do not ever get past that point and carry the mentality of youth forward into full adulthood where it looks stupid to a further progressed onlooker. My philosophy indicates that a balance should be sought, between the material needs of a personality and the spiritual requirements of a soul, until it becomes obvious that the twin turrets of philanthropy and altruism are the senior reasons, *at present*, for incarnate existence.

Few people realise exactly what happens when a desire is created. They are often able to discern good and bad atmospheres but rarely venture to explore just *how* they are created. Let me explain ... firstly, life is not just a three dimensional existence; it comprises of the spirit world which does not live but is life, beneath which are the souls, controlling as part of their evolution and learning process of experience gathering, a mental body. Now, for me that is where the world of primary principles ceases, and we then must enter an area comprised of sub principles, which have forced their way into our consciousness through human fixation with them.

Whatever you habitually think about ... you are! This is a microcosm of what happens when any cosmic mental body fixates on anything. The mass of mental bodies, or minds, which are humanity, began playing with denser creations; etheric vehicles were created which should merely have been light bodies reflecting the purer essence of the soul which created them. Denser forms were contemplated, and over the millennia came into being just as will anything contemplated for long enough and with sufficient concentration. The physical vehicle or corporeal body arrived and before long we were no longer aware of the light body ... but stranger things were at hand ... the friction of the mental body inter-playing with this physical vehicle produced a human desire for desire, the product of which is something that has come to be known as the astral body, desire body or emotional vehicle. This has now become quite confused with the etheric body which is in actual fact the fourth dimension; this dimension, increasing numbers of us are sensing with greater physical awareness as time progresses. I am not writing here about abstract bodies. Everything beneath that level of spirit is dense and can be contacted by physical means, and this etheric body I am describing can actually be seen by many ordinary people.

When making a wish, you actually create immediately in the ether waves, exactly what you are desiring. Nothing more, nothing less. It actually comes into existence contiguously with the denser physical universe. If you were focused in your etheric vehicle you would have this creation instantaneously. It takes a while longer however, for this contiguous creation in ether to manifest in its denser form. Most people loose concentration and bits of desire are created; minds are changed and others become attracted to bits of desire and when successful, total creations. Creators become attracted to their creations, and further on down the line actually become the effect of them.

All of this creation becomes what we now know as the astral plane; an area surrounding our planet of every little thought ever contemplated by the slowly evolving mind of humanity. How come we were able to create so powerfully at the beginning of evolution and not so powerfully here in what perhaps may be described as the middle? Because in the beginning there was a purity without experience. We became involved with this planet, hit a nadir of density from which we now evolve with a consciousness of ourselves. When that power is regained it will be with a responsibility not possible without the human experience. It is therefore currently a much diluted inherent human capacity to create at will.

Meanwhile we are plagued by desire. The astral world has become the whole universe for many who live an existence of emotional *reactions,* without ever contemplating the capacity for mental *action*. When first they contact their minds, the immediate impulse is to wish for something, desire a possession or demand a satisfaction. This is the way it is ... not right ... not wrong ... it just *is* this way. All I seek to explain in this section of the book, is the mess that occurs through irresponsible creation, demand, wish or desire. The astral plane, on which lives all of this creation, demand, wish and desire, is a bad atmosphere, just like the microcosmic one you experience when entering a room where you are not wanted. It does not have to be this way though. Try flowing love into it for example, as a unifying thought.

The shining light film of the ether waves, when exposed to your thoughts, records them just like a digital compact disc or analogue magnetic tape, or indeed any recording medium. Those accessing the ether waves, can play this shining light film, and for some of us, just like the television on in the background of many sitting rooms, it is playing for them randomly, remotely controlled by others, and the recipient of the astral confusion cannot find the off switch.

What will your new shining light film album resemble ... a Beethoven concerto or a psycho-babblic crescendo of unending bedlamic pictures, sounds, feels and confusion, tearing at the heart of any soul daring to tune in. Be careful ... there exists in this piece much useful information which can be used selfishly just as it can be utilised as intended ... for the benefit of all.

Make your choice then ... go on!

INNO AND THE GRAIN OF PARADISE

The problem with drugs is that they are poisonous to the human body. All drugs! In fact anything that does not already exist within you naturally, or is able to be assimilated by you easily, and in harmony with the body's purpose, function and biological constituents, is harmful. Yet, the world is becoming addicted to drugs, both socially, and more surprisingly, medicinally!

Why anyone would wish to quaff a poisonous potion, with side effects because it is poisonous, to alleviate what often amounts to a psychosomatic condition, in preference to spending a little more time and effort researching the illness and discovering what will naturally cure it, be that cure a few wise words from one who knows, or Auntie Willa's herbal remedy, if the condition is indeed of purely physical origin, I find a challenge to understand ... but understand I must for it is the way of the world, which I seek to serve as best I can.

Whilst on vacation in the tropics, Inno met a person called Cardamom. They became friends and Cardamom offered Inno a tablet ... "to experience the true beauty of your surroundings" ... as Cardie so poetically yet inaccurately put it. The aromatic fragrance of Inno's new friend, from which Cardie had been named, became an outrageously wonderful sound, after Inno had taken the pill.

"I will call what you have given me A Grain Of Paradise," Inno stated to Cardie, as the harmony between them grew rampantly by the second. That day passed by, another came, and with it one more grain of paradise from Cardie. They both stayed awake forever and Inno wrote a poem …

The sea becomes silver, the clouds becomes gold,
The forest invites, whoever is told …
About what happens when taking a grain,
Of Paradise being a land without pain.

You taste all the sound and you hear the flavour
You touch the intangible sights which you savour
You think in your foot and you walk on your head
You wonder what happens when life becomes dead

What seems upside down is in fact downside up
The curves are all straight and the squares have three sides
Triangles have radii and everything rhymes
And all this on one grain of paradise!!!

… and then Innominate awoke … "I have had the strangest dream," began Inno in reply to my *good morning,* "and in it occurred the most delightful of experiences, unfortunately stimulated by a drug which I called A GRAIN OF PARADISE. This set me thinking ... if I was able to experience these things which I wrote in a poem during that dream and recalled first thing this morning, it must be that such things are available for my experience anyway. The images which I encountered, must be from within my own universe, for in that universe I remained during this drug experience.

If I can ponder, imagine, mentally create, conceive of, hypothesise about, postulate and mentally assume anything, then it must follow that I can physically accomplish these exact same things. So, if me and a drug can have these wild times, it follows that me and me can too, or indeed me and you ... without the poisonous artificial stimulant.

Stimulants can only invigorate what is already there!

That is some cognition," concluded Inno.

This in turn set me thinking, firstly about my ethics concerning the relating of Inno's dream, *to relate or not to relate was the question,* and secondly as ever, about the relevance of it as an aid to another revelation of human potential. Well, my first concern was easy to override ... I feel that it is best never to withhold information, which, whether valuable or not personally, could prove a vital link in the dawning of a new horizon for others; secondly, regarding human potential, this type of experience is obviously helpful, unless encountered by those who wish to remain entrapped in a three dimensional consciousness .... then there is a third ... Inno mentioned *staying awake forever,* which is the same idea as *continuity of consciousness,* an ultimate in personal development eh? STAYING AWAKE FOREVER ... *realising your full potential even when asleep* ... worthy subject matter for a book itself don't you think?

So, quite where Innominate's grain of paradise episode takes us no one can be sure. But it exists, and not just within Inno's universe! Many of us have experienced wild notions and vivid superhuman ideas, and up until very recently, except for the odd poet, writer, artist or philosopher, we have had nothing to which we could relate our experiences. Now, utilising the YOU AND ME MAKE THREE philosophy, we can further explore the seemingly ridiculous, if we so desire.

If every living soul on planet earth agreed about any one thing, would that one thing become physical fact? Yes, I venture, *yes yes yes!* This planet and its life is nothing more than an agreement. If every single actuality connected with this planet ignored it, then earth would disappear, would it not? If we all visualised world peace, then I guarantee that peace would be immediately apparent at that moment in time of the group visualisation. Agreement begins in your home universe, it seeks life in the 1+1=3 equation, and eventually grows in the manner of compound interest on an overdraft, though a far more pleasant aspect of this phenomenon must be conceptualised if you are to make it agreeable to your life's operating mechanism!

Your visualisation will manifest physically in a time span relating proportionally to the power of your thoughts. If another human mind visualises the same thing, the multiplication of power equation should be obvious. You see 1+1=3, but 3+3=9 and 9+9=27, and this is a simplistic viewpoint not considering all of the 4+7's and 278's+32's.

Inno and I hypothesised for many hours on this matter as we hope you now do. While you are at it you may like to join us in an idea ...

Visualise World Peace ... Together ... With Love

... "that would make an excellent car bumper sticker," concluded Inno.

Thought Control

So the rap began with a discussion about the field of entertainment and its purpose in relation to personal development. Stage trickery, sleight of hand, conjuring, escapology … *escapology?* Harry Houdini's name inevitably crops up during such discussions, but our concentration fell onto a friend of his called Joseph Dunninger.

This guy Dunninger focused his professional life onto thought reading. Houdini, a role model in his time, had created an atmosphere throughout his sphere of influence that did not allow an acceptance of psychic phenomena, and this meant that Dunninger affirmed thought reading as a simple physical attribute accessible by anyone with the necessary apparatus, in this case a brain. This is in line with my own ponderings on the subject and my attention consequently sharpened onto what was being said.

Dunninger had pre-empted my own viewpoint with descriptions of just how such thought reading can be accomplished. Clarity of purpose and concentration are two ingredients; willingness by reader and broadcaster is helpful, and an honourable purpose or clean heart is most desirable, the latter being my addition to the debate.

Now it seems that if you have someone mock up a blackboard, or in these modern times, a television screen, and think onto that screen whatever it is they wish you to read, and you also mock up a television screen and allow that image to fall onto your screen, you are then involved in the simple process of thought reading. There is nothing which remotely falls into the modern definition of psychism there now really ... is there! No goblins, witches or new age spooks telling you about your future for a few quid.

I asked if clarity of thought by the broadcaster would render such readings easier for the receiver and the consensus was that most people's thoughts are chaotic and quite hazy. I suggested that we contemplate an emulation of some computer software that I use which takes an image, and by understanding its patterns, enhances it thereby producing a clearer representation. I said that we could do the same with hazy thoughts we are trying to read as a kind of service to the thinker ... *what should we call it,* asked Ginger; *inter-something,* replied Dreamy ... THE THOUGHT BUREAU, I suggested, *no I have it,* interrupted Dreamy ... *INTER-FERE!*

Yet again, we entered the area of thought control and I could not help but affirm my own feelings written as far back as in my first book, that *thought management* is a prerequisite to all types of personal development. If you cannot control your own modus operandi, how on earth can you be effective in life? Now, Houdini died in 1926 and Dunninger much later in 1956, so do not think for one moment that all of our contemplations about this aspect of human potential are new. We may add a modern slant to the ongoing investigations, but plenty have been at it before us, and it is this previously learned expertise that we can use in our own onward progress, hopefully without the pain; the pain of anything need only be endured once at any point in humanity's evolution. The fact that we constantly feel a need to experience the pain that someone else has kindly undergone for us is indeed a human failing.

The topic of Neuro Linguistic Programming was raised ... as often happens ... much to the irritation of a group member who at that point could not feel the need to discuss *another* non spiritual topic. We talked of Nico's experience with empathy training during the 1960's, and likened it to mirroring in NLP ... the question was ... if you mirror every single little thing in someone you are trying to copy, will this physical mirroring eventually lead to some kind of access into their brain? I think so!

If you copy the world's greatest skier and become adept yourself, because you have not really achieved such progress organically from within, will your next lifetime see you beginning all over again? It seems that this is the case for progress of a spiritual nature made by undergoing any kind of initiation at the hands of a guru, rather than from an understanding within.

Houdini decried psychic phenomena, yet it transpired that he was a Freemason who had a pact with his wife to contact her after his death, which apparently he did. Magicians the world over still hold seances on his deathday in the hope of contact. His stage image of *ultimate escape by physical means* it seems, was different to the man himself. This is in itself a clouding on the subject we call *clarity of thought*. If you attempt a tuning to someone who is duplicitous, no matter how innocuous, will you be capable of translating that duplicity?

Gradual graduation should see you involve yourself carefully in any investigation concerning thought control. Do not try to accomplish everything at once. Instant gratification has an attraction, but in this area it is wise to be happy with an acceptance of deferred gratification for your efforts. Do not seek the sensational, but for the purpose of human evolution, find a like minded friend who is willing to experiment with you in this field.

Way back in the early 1970's, I lived in a bedsit. In the adjacent room lived a friend of mine ... we had attended the same school, were both in different rock bands and had similar interests. We frequently played chess into the small hours whilst discussing the paranormal, which fascinated us both. One particular night, probably after reading something fictional like Dennis Wheatley's THE HAUNTING OF TOBY JUG, we decided to experiment. We would retire and communicate with each other telepathically! There was no plan, no structure to the experiment, no purpose bar curiosity, no preordained formula, no real expectations and consequently no results ... *that we were conscious of,* and it is this last point if utilised as differentiation, that will help you enormously.

Whether or not you agree, all humans are telepathic ... we have the equipment in the neo cortex part of the brain, which has mysteriously *not* been forever present, to both transmit and receive, and these two aspect of telepathy are occurring for you right now as you read these words. How conscious you are of these transmission is the subject of this offering in YOU AND ME MAKE THREE. It is this consciousness which you must foster if telepathy is to become an available tool in your own personal development. All the time you seek some kind of sensational revelation of the Biblical variety, you will be unaware of the reality, which most of us find to be, in the beginning, a dim awareness of another, and before too long, this haziness becomes as vivid as you feel it is safe to allow. The control remains with you at all time and my advice if I was an advice giver, which I am not, would be to drop your defences and get sensitive to thought.

When you develop this latent human power, chuck out the fax, telephone, television, radio and Internet kit ... fascinating though are all of them, they exist in actual fact merely as lower physical harmonics of the human potential which lurks within us all ... this is the personal development in which I deal ... Houdini and Dunninger would approve, and this will get you en route to real power!

INNOMINATE'S MAGIC THREES

Gambling is a way of life for many. Check out Hong Kong; old and young Hongkongese love a game of mah-jong and adore a day, (or week) at the races … reintegration with mainland China has done little to alter that as a way of life, so far. The chance of *anything* seems exhilarating for many, whereas the certainty of something can be boring, at least after a feeling of security has been initially experienced perhaps.

I remember performing in a musical play for a six month tour of Great Britain. It had been an ambition of mine to land the type of role which I was given in this production, and as it happened, I landed the part through a fellow actor defaulting on his contract. I was therefore given only three days rehearsal to learn and perfect a part in a play for which my fellow cast members had been practising around three months. With much help I bluffed my way through the first few nights, frequently singing my lines phonetically rather than lyrically. The lady playing my wife pulled me around the dance routines and a few of my lines were kindly delivered by proxy!

After two weeks on tour, (don't ever think that type of life is easy!) I perfected my portrayal of the character whom I represented, and with a month of performances behind me the boredom crept through the stage door and into my dressing room. What seemed insurmountable with three days to opening, then resembled thespian purgatory, as I had polished not only my part, but also learnt some of the other roles which I began aspiring towards portraying, and did not set any other goal for myself in that show. Of course I continued with a professional outlook on this situation, but I here share my hitherto private thoughts about it with you.

A buzz for me came with the uncertainty, and boredom arrived once all was known and understood. This is but a microcosm of the much vaster idea we call evolution … *learning through incarnate experience.* If we knew it all, as some believe they do, (and me also as a younger person) then I cannot presently conceive of another raison d'être, or reason for life, except perhaps for that brief glimpse of certainty before the boredom sets in.

Inno told me of a personal idiosyncrasy which had caused it many hours of pondering … "every time I throw the dice, I land the magic threes. If I throw a die singly, the result is random; whenever I throw a pair however, the magic threes appear. This means that I cannot ever indulge in a game requiring the throwing of two dice, for it will always be within my power to win if two threes can be called as a bet."

"Are you not tempted to make yourself comfortable for this life through profit from this idiosyncrasy, thus allowing you to better serve fellow souls?" I questioned naively.

"I thought you would ask that," continued Inno, "for such response is but human. Whatever the definitive answer however, my explanation is that I cannot. Nevertheless, it is through pondering this idea that I have been able to achieve a degree of understanding regarding the human lot of walking this earth, and I can see by your expression that you would not mind me sharing this comprehension with you … we may discover an interesting gestalt in the merging of our two viewpoints, for I know that is your purpose in this latest book you are writing.

Simply, my postulate was this … if humanity was able to put survival onto automatic pilot, then it could evolve far easier as a creative species. Yet, the paradox of this conjecture is that some of the finest creations we have, evolved from a cope situation, poverty, hunger or bankruptcy. So what would happen if the automatic pilot turned us all into a bunch of dithering idiots, languishing in our indolence and wasting for want of purpose? My magic threes are your wonderful Family, for I do not possess such an asset. You may not see your Family in this light, but my external viewpoint is able to afford such comprehension. You threw the dice and manifested an incredible wife, an understanding son, a caring daughter, a faithful dog and a thankful cat ... *for he was a last chance stray!*

I have heard you lean towards a moan regarding the size of your house and scarcity of disposable income, yet to me, these moans are your magic threes. The scarcity you mention is an abundance to most, just as the scrapings from your plate would feed a starving refugee from the third world.

All is relative and *your* relatives are all!

Now, what I propose as a good idea, is to understand what are your assets, and boring or not, preserve them, thus affording yourself time and space to pursue a creative life. This type of creativity is not restricted to art, music or writing; it is the creation of *life itself.* If you are forever seeking your next meal, or your next million, it must be said, you will be unable to pursue life's creative opportunities. To plagiarise and adapt a phrase from YOU CAN ALWAYS GET WHAT YOU WANT ...

it is easier to create with a pound in your pocket, than it is on an empty stomach

... so the magic threes are that pound in your pocket and you are now able to peruse opportunity with discretion and a degree of freedom."

"I see what you mean," I began, "and can vouch for the fact that when I have been fortunate enough to encounter a fellow human who is actually living life creatively, it is a most incredible experience on par with any song-writing, story-writing, play-writing, artistic idea or feeling I have ever had. In fact I find these people far more intriguing than the orthodox creative arts, for I have mastered much relevant expertise in such established creative art, yet in the art of living I am but a neophyte!"

Inno added with gusto ... "slipping a piece of bread into the toaster is art to people of that kind, and a few words of social intercourse between two such people is to them akin to your favourite classical symphony.

Life is art and art is life."

"The greatest conventional artists merely communicate some aspect of life in a pleasing way," I added.

"Art is the soul of the world.

Why are artists as people, so rarely as good as the art they create?"

"Because they *are* people and subject to the restrictions of an incarnate physical life. When allowed to create in the mental universe there are no such restrictions," answered Inno.

"So it follows that the greatest artists are those who have been able to present the maximum amount of abstraction to a physical audience in a pleasing format," I announced.

"Perhaps," concluded Inno.

Discover your magic threes and work out a modus operandi around them, he, she or it. Get creative with all that you contemplate and act upon. Inno's magic threes were never used to its advantage, and this was the advantage to Inno of having them. Inno sees my Family as magic threes, just as I see your present situation containing so many throws of happy dice that I wonder why you have ever questioned your serendipitous circumstances. All is not perpetually as it seems when looking beyond the obvious to new horizons. Most of us will have pragmatic magic threes which can act as the engine room for a creative life … use them.

Oh, and talking of families …

FAMILIES
And How To Thrive In Them

I was involved with writing and research for the book which will follow this one, called STAYING AWAKE FOREVER. This work is about continuity of consciousness, and as you may already have gathered it is quite a complex subject involving much postulating, occasional results and a depth of involvement rarely accomplishable in the hustle bustle atmosphere of our modern day world.

For me it was the most rewarding task in which I could be absorbed; working out how to achieve greater gain from the one third of our lives we think is currently inaccessible. *True personal development,* I felt. *Absorbed* was certainly the word to describe my condition however. The business from which I partially draw my income was suddenly expanded during the same time period. Stock was increased, staff recruited, new offices inhabited and a large publicity campaign for my work was instigated for the first time.

With outgoings exceeding income, it was realised that we must seek interest from the mass media to heighten general awareness, *(new-speak for boosting sales!)* and hired a publicist, who immediately tuned into the most newsworthy portion of my work; what I say in YOU CAN ALWAYS GET WHAT YOU WANT about visualising yourself with *loads of cash* if that is what you want. The largest selling daily tabloid in Britain bought into the story and negotiated the inclusion of portions from that book into a serialisation. Also at the same time, sales for our Russian translation of the same book began to boom, and I was asked to make live presentations in both St Petersburg and Moscow.

YOU CAN ALWAYS GET WHAT YOU WANT was written as the first book of a series and outlines a very physical and personality based route to success ... still valid, in fact more so now than at any other time, and I have no doubt this validity will continue to climb for this product over the coming 150 years or so. Regardless of this, the mind was elsewhere, thoughts otherwise engaged and my focus lay in the depths of potential not relevant to the mentioned interest in the also mentioned first book.

As I prepared the presentation for Russia and my tactics for the tabloid dailies, I realised that I had become so divorced from these initial success routes that I ran the risk of being totally ineffective! I was being asked to teach *loadsamoney* potential from a continuity of consciousness perspective and this was a strain. I pondered the situation and cognited ...

the message platform is more important than the message.

"It is no use having something good to say if there is not a comparable platform from which to say it," I stated repeatedly to whoever would listen, as I struggled to maintain a connection with the real world of arguments, disagreements, fighting, speaking with forked tongues, making money, value judgements, physical love, sex, unemployment, disgruntlement, expectations and membership of families!

Whilst all of the above was occurring, it transpired that an extended family member from another country, whom I had been unable to see during a previous visit because of commitments, had been visiting the remainder of the family elsewhere for the previous two weeks. No telephone call as was usual had been forthcoming to announce the presence, so I realised that there was an upset. I called and was asked if I had not received an Email some weeks prior, to which I honestly replied in the negative. Technological failure, we both concluded; there was still upset, but I left it, even with the philosophy of *communication being a panacea for all upsets,* I deemed it relevant to allow a *passage of time healing* for that particular episode and mismanaged communication. Another closer member of my family disagreed.

I changed the approach whilst considering my potential for insensitivity, by calling again and asking once more if there was an upset. Now, let me be quite plain about the fact that there *was* an upset … that is not the question … what we are discussing here is how to *thrive* as a family member. Four of my family had bitched, moaned, criticised, bestowed value judgements and opinions upon me in great quantities, in my absence, and this information was embarrassingly withheld from me. It was uncomfortable but not uncontrollable. We can call this action of theirs A KEEP BACK.

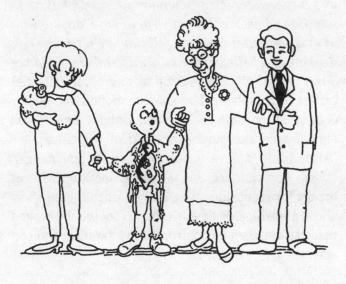

Now, the moment I probed with questions any deeper than the superficial, that KEEP BACK became a MISSED KEEP BACK. They are the dangerous ones. Boy, watch out for those little devils because they can hit you right between the eyes spontaneously and cause indescribable damage which may remain irreparable for a lifetime. A MISSED KEEP BACK is a KEEP BACK whose keeper is not sure if you know about it.

As I trawled back over my recent time track, I remembered a number of instances which could have been responsible for such upset and quoted them as possibilities. *Not enough acknowledgement for a recently born baby, inability to collect people from the airport, refusing sleeping accommodation to someone whom we did not wish to have staying with us at a particular time, not telephoning often enough, working in a field which was alien to others, adopting direct ways of communication,* were all potential causes of complaint. The human emotion and poorly controlled response told me that without doubt I was almost accurate, but in the case of a MISSED KEEP BACK, being almost accurate is the actual danger. Unless you can clear the whole business up without breaks for reconsideration, do not touch the area and allow a *passage of time healing* to soothe the wound before it can then be confronted in a far more indirect way.

For a considerable number of years previous to this episode, I had been most definitely working very much from a soul perspective, then suddenly I was thrust into the world of personalities, and the shock for me was, that I was thrown at all. I regained stability, but I had been thrown. It will not happen again because of the strength which is now mine forever due to this upset. Although we are all still friends, the conclusion for that episode saw my wife and I sitting in a service meditation, flowing love to all parties concerned. Now, I say service meditation, which it most certainly was, but let me further qualify that description by saying that the immediate result of that service was a return of serenity for us. The others would have benefited in their own ways also.

Always turning such situations into advantage, I asked myself what had been the benefits gained, but they became obvious as I applied myself to the new presentations for Russia and my interviews for the tabloids with renewed and revigourated purpose. The episode had grounded me, giving me an increased usefulness in my job. I understood the need for YOU CAN ALWAYS GET WHAT YOU WANT once again.

As for thriving within a family, it is important to understand the following ... family are not necessarily friends, but hopefully so; physical showerings of emotional love have little to connect them to a universal flowing of real soul love into the ether which surrounds our planet; one cannot hide pretentiously behind spiritual service as an excuse for unconnectedness and uselessness to physical life; grant space and beingness for others to *be how they are* and not as you expect them to be; quantity of communications are rarely related to quality of communications ... just sometimes; if you continue to make people uncomfortable in your presence, family or not, they will refrain from purposely seeking your company; if there is an upset and someone gives you the opportunity to voice that upset, take it, and do not make them wrong by lying through saying there is nothing wrong when there is ... it is even worse to behave in this way with someone who is actively practising intuition; do not take selfish advantage of physical family membership, and remember *the emotional bank account,* deposit more than you withdraw; if you are aware of telepathy, remember that what you sense is not necessarily what you wish to sense!

I have no upset with anyone in this universe ... I love my family and friends along with a renewed acquaintance called YOU CAN ALWAYS GET WHAT YOU WANT. There are many different ways of remaining friends, and sometimes the choice must be to avoid intimate company with some. Telephone friendships are possibilities for many families to remain familiar, whilst for others, if too much compromise is too frequently required, wedding and funeral meetings seem to be the most appropriate form of contact.

If we consistently bestow our personal reality as an expectation of others, family or not, the chances of achieving lasting friendship and universal service are almost nil ... so thrive and don't do it!

INNOMINATE STANDS FOR PARLIAMENT

This book was written during the year of a British General Election. 1997. Such a political procedure is designed to allow the population to select who will represent them in THE MOTHER OF ALL PARLIAMENTS, as the House of Commons has been referred to many times. This House is not dissimilar to the House of Representatives in the United States of America although it has the power of the American Congress, which perhaps the House of Lords was designed to have, but thankfully does not.

Many national governments have been moulded on the British system; with the advantage of being able to judge the flaws in our legislative method, apparent improvements have been made in many, as have quite a few systems sadly fallen into disarray. It seemed to me that a wise thing like Innominate would make tremendous contributions to our political platform if it would agree to offer itself as a candidate for Member of Parliament.

"Will you?" I asked.

"Of course not," was the quick response, "what do you take me for? You have seen and listened to those people who are best suited for this job you mention ... do I fit into that category?"

"That is the whole idea," I interrupted, "you would make the difference ... you would instigate powerful changes ... you would be the example ... you could be a prime minister!"

"Nonsense," insisted Inno, "do you know what originality is? It is the power of creating freshly with newness. It is not derivative or imitative; it is first-hand and spontaneous. I am those things. Politics is not. Join the two together and a collision occurs. That is not good and nor is it your intention I know. Let us therefore examine how we can best effect powerful change for the better in this society of which we are part.

Firstly, let me tell you that society's understanding of originality is extremely limited to say the least. The concept has become defined within the comfort zone acceptable to our community. In other words, if I were to perform an absolutely original act, such as dancing naked whilst singing angel chants on the hustings, to represent the birth of a new opportunity in politics, I would be arrested and examined for mental illness; yet, a politician may debate the pros and cons of allowing a nation to starve, whilst our own European warehouses are so stuffed with food we create mountains and lakes of perishables which we frequently destroy to preserve the economic status quo.

Then we call that sanity!

Where do I fit into that framework my friend? I do, but not in the way you have suggested. There is no better industry to illustrate our understanding of originality than the popular music business in which you spent so many of your formative years. The follow up song to a hit record will do nicely for our purpose. It is frequently only a slight change from that which has already been approved by the public, who voted with their purses through buying the first product. The record companies do not like too many changes for the follow up as that could alienate the audience. A recording is therefore "fabricated" with marketing in mind, and called original.

David Bowie was thought of as an original artist when he introduced his alter ego Ziggy Stardust to us in the early seventies. Yet, he would be the first to admit that this character was but a theatrical creation singing basic rock n' roll melodies with lyrics occasionally referring to space. Now, *this* is what society understands as original, but that does not mean it is original. Actually the popular understanding of originality, is a form of union containing already existing actualities. The Beatles did the same by synthesising what had gone before, straining it through their collective beingness, before offering us another excellent example for our erroneous understanding of originality ... enjoyable nevertheless!

The Beatles even got caught occasionally when their new offerings were not dissimilar enough from what had gone before. The song Come Together is an example, and the later George Harrison composition called My Sweet Lord, which was musically very similar to an earlier song called He's So Fine. *(doo lang doo lang doo lang)*

So, we have our definition of originality in order have we not?"

"Yes," I began answering, but Inno was hot to continue; who was I to stop such a rich flow of helpful philosophy.

"You see," continued Inno, aware that I'd had something to add but withheld it for the purpose of helping the general drift, "the British parliamentary system is original from an historical perspective, where dictators, be they kings, queens or commoners, were the norm. We are merely coming to terms with democracy, which, by its very nature, demands an exploration of extraordinary length, before finally mastering it, at which time it becomes obsolete, for any people able to master democracy is also able to evolve onward from it, perhaps to a system of self government from within each individual.

You do this already, as does your friend who calls himself a Silent Knight. Both of you are aware of the societal need to exist between the excruciatingly narrow confines of group legislation, yet really you govern yourselves from within, often adding structures to your own lives which go way beyond the current societal necessity, and often flaunting more common agreements when ridiculous.

Of this modus operandi I am approving, but do not think that the likes of us can stride into Parliament and be understood, for this would be foolish; nor do I feel this to be the case within your ideas. Real power is hidden; it is occult ... it contains an understanding of energy flows and an awareness of useful manipulation for the common good. This effective orchestration cannot be accomplished exoterically at present. The conductor must remain invisible.

I am a conductor and there are many more powerful conductors far more efficacious than I, all around the world, probing the minds of statespeople whatever their political persuasion. Just as you have inspired stories, songs and philosophy from the omnipresent and omniscient ether waves, often knowingly, so too do politicians and bureaucrats, civil servants and business people, wherever they exist, inspire, *mainly unwittingly,* ideas, be they good or bad, from the exact same space!

Someone or something must originate those ideas for them to be synthesised and called original by their recipients, and this energy I transmit continuously, even as I speak these words to you for your new book. Your friend who calls himself a Silent Knight, flows universal love and forgiveness into this space I speak about, and this helps quieten the appalling din of want and greed which exists all around the planet on an astral plane, intended as a forum for the exhibition of *love as the unifying principle of existence,* yet utilised by humans currently for sexual, financial and personality type expression of a greedy nature.

Such is life … at present that is!

So my friend, for every powerful individual visible in this world, there is an invisible helper continuously expiring a flow of ideas available for such a person to inspire as an original thought. Sometimes of course, and it has to be said, the evil discarnate and incarnate get their way using this occult knowledge, and something ugly happens which makes us question the existence of any god concept!

Currently, there is a balance tipped in the favour of good, and this makes me feel that opportunities, not only for the next British Parliament, but the coming two thousand years for the whole planet, are excellent. The idea of democracy is an evolving relevance and not totally dissimilar to your Positive Attitude Club. Parliament is a forum where human viewpoints may be aired without qualification excepting suppressions self imposed by each member for selfish ends. It is just a long and often arduous process.

Will I offer myself as a candidate for Parliament?

No!

Innominate stands for Parliament. Innominate stands for freedom. Innominate stands for good. Innominate stands for progress. Innominate stands for charity. Innominate stands for justice. Innominate stands for love. Innominate stands for … well … everything that would spoil if I stood physically as a candidate for Parliament!"

Stock Letter From A Silent Knight

It may come as a shock for some regular readers of these books, to discover that my friend a Silent Knight is alive and well, living in the United States of America. He has his fair share of challenges, as do we all, and lives an exemplary life of service prescribed by himself through philosophy outlined in earlier books. His particular approach to living may sound at times cynical to some, but he is now quite old, in his eighties in fact, with *time on his hands and nothing more to prove,* as he puts it, and I find his viewpoints particularly effective and refreshing.

I have pow-wowed with him many times on a wide diversity of topics; he gets crotchety like the rest of us, when common sense does not seem to prevail in this world, but like I said, he has time on his hands to put little things right when he can. This he has accomplished admirably by replying to one of those sick type personalised mailers we all receive once in a while, in his own inimitable way. Because this *letter from Ashley* is one which promises results related to the world of personal development, a world for which I take responsibility whenever it is within my sphere of influence, I feel an urge to shout *beware,* not just of this one letter containing spiritual promises to which the following is a reply, but all of the other magical personal development promises which are waiting in envelopes to be mailed to us with one purpose only in mind ... *to make money for the sender!*

A Silent Knight's reply is included as part of You AND ME MAKE THREE, because it is walking the talk of personal development, which states that not only do we celebrate all that is good with this world, but occasionally we have to get down to the business of putting certain aspects right when they have departed from rationality, or just *plain gone off the rails,* as SK would say.

A Silent Knight and myself would be particularly pleased if you felt an urge to copy this letter, or better still just use it as a model, and send it or similar as a reply to like letters which instigated this one. Such letters you will receive, of that fact I am not in doubt. You can imagine what the original *letter from Ashley* stated and I will not overcrowd this book with the unnecessary verbiage which was contained therein.

Dear Ashley,

As you have apparently "chosen" me with such concern, I in turn have been called to send you this *very personal letter,* which I hope you will take the time to read, as I did yours. This letter which you are now reading, is my new stock letter to reply to communications such as yours, and is merged to a mailing list which I made from all such letters as is the type you have just sent me. Your name can be embedded in as many places as I choose, without much effort from me and thanks to the technology of computers and their software, making it appear even more personal. At least I  am being honest about that. What you have sent me is accomplished quite easily by anyone with a computer, and any software that executes merge mailing.

Being especially selected, as you imply I was, is as easy as buying mailing lists which have been filtered by categories of interest, like Astrology, Numerology, Metaphysics, Mysticism, Personal Development, Esotericism, for "hot names and addresses." You know that and I know that, but I'm receiving an average of 3 to 5 such letters a week and I am tired of my attention being forced onto such sad manipulations of our modern communication potentials! In fact I once received 6 in one day!

Ashley, I have been an Astrologer, Mystic and

involved in just about any type of mind control, spiritual meditation, divination, prayer, and personal development you can name for over 40 years, both in intense theoretical studies and solid practice. I have been blessed and am fortunate enough that I don't need to sell my spiritual capabilities which have been developed to a degree at least equal to most psychics of which I am aware; I am developing certain powers such as clairvoyance, the ability to astral travel, power to influence others, and practice simple telepathy. I am very aware, as I trust you are, of the consequences when using these abilities for self aggrandisement or deception, appealing to others for personal gain in the same manner as any material business does, with free gifts, time limits and all sorts of urgings to get that fee in the mail or contact by phone immediately!

If you have any spiritual talents in the metaphysical field Ashley, these were given to you because of your stage in evolution. Any of us who are so blessed should shine upon others who are less gifted, as the sun beams freely on all alike. It is surely so, that if it were possible, someone would find a way to charge us for sun light and the air that we breath; many would jump on the band wagon as psychics have done with 900 numbers. (0800 numbers in the United Kingdom ... Free*fone* ... PM) It is so obviously done for the money, I have to laugh else I cry for those yet unawakened to the power they have within themselves.

Apparently the 900 idea is not as hot now as the increasing numbers of "spiritually talented" persons have found the direct mailing to be, of letters such as yours. This has only mushroomed in the latter part of 1997, so it must promise to be lucrative for those doing it, in addition to this "great personal interest and concern" for the addressee. You all must have bought the same, perhaps discounted, mailing list at about the same time. Not only do the generic phrases which apply to almost any human such as, "life has been hard for you," "you've been unlucky," "unhealthy?" "lonely?" "financially burdened?" ... and other such *shot-gun* type phrases ... not only, I say, do these phrases NOT apply to me, but *they never have!* I've lived a blessed life of health, wealth, and love, the three most common articles trying to be sold for a price! And I didn't have to pay anyone a fee!

In keeping with the Higher Laws, Ashley, it is not my right to judge you or anyone else. Ascended Beings can only, by the Laws concerning Free Will, place knowledge before us, hoping we will choose that which will move us in the direction of "on earth as it is in heaven." This is humanity's purpose for being ... we're the "ground crew," so to speak, for achieving that purpose, and it is especially important at this cosmic moment in time as we are moving into a new dimension on a global basis.

This has been foretold for ages.

If you can't or don't believe it, I am very sorry. All those with special gifts are needed now to use their powers for the help of aspirants having lesser wisdom. "Father forgive them for they know not what they do." Only *you* know in your heart whether you are really helping others develop themselves in Truth or not, with your mailing activity. As it is said, "If the shoe fits, wear it." If it doesn't, then this letter has only been a reminder, and it is hoped you will forgive me.

In my meditations and contacts with Higher Ones, I am directed to send this to anyone selling spiritual advice or professed psychically acquired knowledge for "very especially selected persons," as such activity allies itself with the forces that wish to inhibit the self-development of those seeking higher Truth's, awareness and consciousness. I am doing this after disposing of some 30-40 such letters as yours which should have received this message also by now. *Better late than never,* to utilise a cliché, and as I have now sent this letter to a friend in publishing, I am hoping it receives wider usage than I myself am able to put into practice.

I hope and pray all misusers of modern technology in the name of personal development will receive it from sources other than myself. There is a great battle going on right now for human souls ... there always has been ... but it is now more intense than ever with communication developed to its present world wide extent. *Light-workers* are desperately needed to use their gifted talents to radiate or broadcast into the mental realms of earth, soul-saving thought forms such as LOVE, FORGIVENESS, HARMONY, and PEACE, the needed elements of Heaven-on-Earth which is very close to becoming manifest. It can happen gently if enough think and hold these thought-forms, or with violence and destruction if not.

For only a stamped, self-addressed envelope from you or any you tell of this, I will help you as you have offered to help me, by use of a special computer program, to choose 5 six-digit Lottery numbers which, if played consistently for 12 months, will most assuredly hit at least once during that period. This program is especially structured with guidance from above, and only I have it. I am bound by sacred oath that I cannot use it on myself or anyone close to me. Nor can I sell this service. **I can only participate in 5% of any winnings the participant receives if that participant is so inclined.** *I am not to complain if I receive nothing. The Ascended Ones wish to* *demonstrate true Spiritual Guidance un-motivated by money; because money, being the most portable material object and power on earth, is by its nature the polar opposite to spirituality and has the habit of taking first priority sooner or later on this plane, even when intentions are altruistic.*

Ashley, please accept blessings and divine love from myself, the ascended ones and company of heaven, who are continually showering their love and patience upon earth and children of The Great One, called by many names.

I AM

A messenger

TELLING THE TRUTH HONESTLY

I told a cute little personal story in one of my books regarding a physical challenge with which I was involved. It was about a fistula which appeared in an awkward place ...

> I developed a large lump about one inch from my anus. I attempted to heal it during the first week of its life, but it was just developing towards its peak and seemed in no mood to disappear. I visited my poor National Health Doctor, who had the sad job of examining the area. That is mentioning little of what it was like for me bending over the couch showing all to my more than understanding lady doctor. She pronounced it a fistula, which was an abnormal and swollen narrow duct in my case, and promptly made an appointment for me to see the specialist for such phenomena. I viewed it as a crystallisation of energy which I had been utilising for writing my third personal development book called EMPOWERMENT. Between the two of us, and with help from a strong course of antibiotics, I believed we could encourage it to leave. Meanwhile the pain was excruciating, and it happened to peak during a talk I was pledged to attend. Of course I could not sit upright and this provoked some unusual glances during the meditation which concluded that particular evening. In bed later that night, it burst, and a greenish yellow liquid showed itself.
>
> Around a month later, I eventually saw the specialist, who inserted a probe into the fistula and a

finger ... *or was it an arm* ... into my anus. He looked at me with a smile and said that his finger was touching the end of the probe inside of me ... *it is definitely a fistula,* he concluded.

He described the surgery which would be necessary to heal it, but I had other ideas. I always believed that this body would never need surgery, and I remembered that commitment as he suggested the treatment. I had doubts however, and allowed my name to be placed on his waiting list. After two months I made around six enquiries and no one seemed acquainted with my case. I decided to cure the hole myself. By this time it had become embarrassing. You know what type of material is present in that rear area ... well some of this waste matter was finding its way down my friendly little fistula ... I need describe that no further.

The point is that as soon as I showed resolve and commitment to the cure, it *was* forthcoming. Whilst searching for *cure tools*, I remembered writing, in *Before the Beginning is a Thought,* about the most vital element a human body needs being oxygen. I therefore gave this anal area of mine an external twice daily dose of oxygen using the hair dryer. *"What are you doing,"* asked my daughter one day, *"drying his bum,"* replied her brother on my behalf; *"oxygenating my health challenge,"* I corrected ... *"Oh,"* they both responded quite matter of factly.

A further two months passed before all signs were gone, but *I* cured the problem. It was a sheer coincidence that an appointment for surgery another two months after that, arrived on the morning I saw the doctor about my knee which I had injured whilst laying a path at the side of our house. Naturally I cancelled it and pondered that word *synchronicity*, which a friend of mine who calls himself The Storyteller defines as *"coincidence with meaning."* The strangest thing that happened in connection with this fistula, was that it reappeared immediately after I cancelled the hospital bed for which I had been, or had not been, waiting for around six months. I was warned that cancellation would mean returning to the bottom of the list ... *"I can assure you the bed will not be necessary,"* I guaranteed the nurse! I cured it once again.

Well wasn't I the strong one? The thing is that it once again reappeared following the publication of that book from which the preceding quotation was taken; after suffering it off and on for around two years I requested the operation and was grateful to all concerned who made it happen for me. I was worried that I had transmitted an incomplete communication about my successes and tribulations. This world is full of claims by people less than honest. Whilst it is important for humanity to grasp its own potential, it is harmful when they are constantly confronted with tricks and claims which prove unfounded. Faith may be lost in the possibilities for self improvement!

I had told the truth, yet in order to tell the truth honestly and completely, all those people who crossed my path through reading or listening to the mentioned work which is call THE 49 STEPS TO A BRIGHT LIFE, would need to be contacted for the epilogue of that particular story ... not really possible in our case, and this part of YOU AND ME MAKE THREE is the closest I can get to redressing the incomplete information.

I agreed to the operation on the understanding that I could have it feeling numb after a local anaesthetic had been administered. I am involved with a long term aspiration for what is called *continuity of consciousness,* which is more widely described in the book called STAYING AWAKE FOREVER, and was unsure of my abilities in succumbing to a general anaesthetic physically, whilst remaining spiritually conscious. To tell the truth honestly, I was more than a little scared, and therefore insisted on the local anaesthetic, which turned out to be extremely uncomfortable without doubt. Because the area in which the surgery was to occur was unsuitable for a dental type local injection, I had to have a spinal injection.

Naturally all involved were more than just curious as to why I wanted to be awake, it being normal to be rendered unconscious, and when my knees began to shake as I bent double on the trolley, naked, whilst the anaesthetist and her many female helpers tried to find the relevant part of my spine to inject, and my legs were trussed up into a position with which female readers may be more familiar, before the surgeon was ushered through in true pop star fashion to administer the cut, clamping together and stitching of the offending item, I felt utterly humbled, painfully assaulted and gratefully cured, even though the mess of such an operation stayed with me for the following two months.

So there, I have now told the truth honestly, but there is a deeper message behind the purpose for this chapter and it is this:

Firstly it is *my* truth with which I have been honest!

Truth and honesty are not synonyms for each other!

One may honestly tell a lie … just as it is.

One person's reality is another's abstraction.

Honesty does not only apply to good … one can also be honestly evil.

Truth is axiomatic to this universe and it is only by adopting universal principles within an individual modus operandi, that we will be capable of making larger leaps forward more quickly. *There is no religion higher than truth,* said H P Blavatsky; *and not the other way around,* added Phil Murray. A truth satisfying to those who did not ever feel comfortable with denominational religions which were offered to us as part of the socialisation process, and others who now see the real light! That light which can be made to shine ever brighter inside each and every one of us. That is truth!

Because a new approach to anything, in this case physical curing of a human ailment, does not seem to work totally first time, we must beware of writing off such potential for the future. It is a 21st century offence to ridicule others who are daring enough to bare all for the purpose of progress. Just because the total aspiration for anything is not concluded as intended, do not underestimate the contribution any apparently unrelated efforts did in fact make to the holistic conclusion.

Telling the truth honestly can be divided into two sections for our purposes here ... the first involves your relationship to universal principles ... the second, more relevant to this book, involves the communications between your inner universe of mind, your surrounding environment and other people. Advanced personal developers understand that their psychological truth is not sacrosanct and merely a transient beingness, but it is this transient beingness from which you are communicating in the main, to the world.

If you snarl this transient beingness up with make wrongs and make rights, rules and regulations, profit and loss, good and bad, love and hate and a whole host of other less than beneficial human outlooks, you will not be doing justice to this transient beingness we call a lifetime. Submit your psychology to universal truth and see what happens.

That is the truth!

THE TRUTH BEHIND ALL RELIGIONS

A good friend from America, thoughtful and spiritually advanced well beyond the present norm, Emailed me with a great idea. He had been on vacation in Costa Rica, when he was confronted by a Born Again Christian metaphorically demanding my friend's devotion to the BAC's very divinely anthropomorphic idea of Jesus Christ. My friend has patience for such bigotry and developed the relationship to a point where the BAC presented him with a book called L̲o̲ Q̲u̲e̲ M̲e̲ G̲u̲s̲t̲a̲ D̲e̲ T̲u̲ R̲e̲l̲i̲g̲i̲o̲n̲ ... in English this means, W̲h̲a̲t̲ I̲ L̲i̲k̲e̲ O̲f̲ (A̲b̲o̲u̲t̲) Y̲o̲u̲r̲ R̲e̲l̲i̲g̲i̲o̲n̲. This inspired my friend to ponder *the one truth behind all religions* and any

effect such a discovery would have upon humanity. He obviously utilises similar philosophy to that which I carry with me ... transmuting all less than harmonious circumstances to both personal and interpersonal advantage!

The truth behind all religions however, is a flawed supposition in that there is not necessarily one in existence, but nevertheless a search for which, many have made and more have contemplated making. If a religion was to base itself on pure truth, it would instantaneously become obsolete as it handed over power from itself to its adherents, and its philosophy would become extinguished as it was exactly duplicated in understanding by those placing attention on it. This is based on the postulate that to replicate something exactly would make it disappear, but let us not become pedantic to the point of uselessness here!

If Christianity was based on Christ, it would only sanction love blended with wisdom; churches would have little or no usefulness as the trend to be seen going to these buildings for the purpose of worship became embarrassing. Basing Buddhism on Buddha would only attract those seeking truth through personal enlightenment. There would not be much of a social game in that because you can do it yourself ... there is no one to disagree with, argue with or lecture ... except yourself that is.

If you are seeking *the one truth* then it is not possible and you will be unsuccessful, for the many roads which lead to Rome are the seven rays of energy which serve this planet and from which all is formed. This entails many differing routes home towards truth for as wide a diversity of people as is humanity. We can consequently and crudely divide humanity into seven sections which correspond to the seven mentioned rays of energy. I will not complicate this explanation by dwelling on facts like these seven sections are then sub divided into forty nine lesser sections and that the personality, or body can be formed from a different ray to that of the overshadowing soul ... let us here keep simplicity in our hearts for the purpose of self realisation in those who have not yet cognited on just what they are ...

> First ray ... will or power
> Second ray ... love-wisdom
> Third ray ... active intelligence
> Fourth ray ... harmony
> Fifth ray ... concrete knowledge
> Sixth ray ... devotion, idealism
> Seventh ray ... ceremonial order

From these descriptions, together with their sub sections and the intermingling of soul ray with personality ray, can be seen that there is as broad a variance of truth as there are human beings trying to understand truth. In fact truth can be honestly told in so many different ways that eventually it all seems like lies!

This is why Rosicrucianism is good for some, Masonry for others, Christianity of the BAC variety for our already mentioned Costa Rican friend, ancient philosophy, black magic, sex magic, yogas, materialism, hatred, mysticism, science, love and war for many ... Theosophy and Esotericism for me, including all of Alice Bailey's books written in conjunction with the Tibetan Master Djwhal Khul and perpetuated by The Lucis Trust. Some of these philosophies are almost basics, unlike mine which is just a personal dip into many pots with a resultant diluted presentation of all, to you, of what was there found and synthesised through me and my own experiences ... this is more or less what my books and audios are incidentally, with the exception of STAYING AWAKE FOREVER which has some new ground in it, yet also blended from a variety of sources.

The only purpose for me writing these books is however, to inspire readers, and listeners when an audio is involved, to look within and discover themselves and remind them of the fact that they can do without me! I have no desire to be considered original, for no such concept exists except in theory, unless originality is merely the blending of what is all around, in our own special way. The main reason people buy my work is that they would find my sources unpalatable in their original state, yet know inherently that the ideas are good and acceptable when inspired then assimilated by me, blended and philosophised before being regurgitated with understanding in a twenty first century format.

The scientific creation of our universe is not what we here ponder, for in that there *is* truth and as exact a modus operandi as there is to be had! This science is more of an occult way of viewing life ... the pondering of God as a concept is very mystical for many, but in the blending of both, you have Esotericism, the combining of heart and head, and if you are able to balance the head and heart in all that you contemplate and do, you will have a greater understanding of life than almost all of humanity that has preceded your particular incarnation.

If there had to be truth behind all religions, then it probably lies in The Old Commentaries, The Upanishads or assorted Hindu scriptures, but the only one I can "understand" is God, which is a concept each must focus on before intuitively sensing what truth there is which calls itself, or which we call, God.

God is the concept we must all ponder at some point in time. There is no escaping it. We are drawn to it like in Greek mythology when the sirens used to lure unwary sailors onto the rocks! Except of course the basic flaw in that analogy which is that the sailors were duped, and it seems the closer we draw ourselves to God the happier or more contented we become, and the greater our understanding is of truth.

The truth behind all religions is not God however ... the truth behind all religions is humanity's manipulation of the God concept. If you want to find real truth then only you can know it. No one can tell you it and it cannot be worded. Wonderful though literature is, the shortcomings of words and their semantics are too great to transmit the finer concepts which at present we are able to experience in a variety of ways, but not accurately relate to others ... we must try however, as it is through the interchange of ideas, the making of personal into transpersonal then interpersonal, the sudden dawning of new horizons after personal cognition with a desire to have others experience their own, the realisation of self and the helping of others to realise themselves, that we will create the new world religion.

When asked what is this new world religion the reply will always be ... *well, what does it mean to you?* A discussion will ensue, your viewpoint plus the other will make another viewpoint, or truth, not readily reducible to its constituent elements. This is the magic of humanity ... the fact that you and me make three!

INNOMINATE TELLS A LIE

All this talk of truth and honesty left Inno with a thirst for the opposite, and this is human nature is it not? *How can you know one without experiencing the other,* was the constant question uppermost in the musings of our champion. HIDING LIES DECEITFULLY and THE FABRICATIONS IN FRONT OF ALL KNOWLEDGE were to have been the corresponding chapters to those two you have just read entitled TELLING THE TRUTH HONESTLY and THE TRUTH BEHIND ALL RELIGIONS, if you are following my words sequentially that is, which is not really important when compared to gaining one fairly weighty cognition realised from any portion or sequence of this work.

So, it seems that aspects of life seemingly opposite to one another, almost meet in concept. Fascism and Communism showed no light between them in practice, and it was noticed that when loving a person from an emotional standpoint, such emotional love often turned into a kind of opposite hatred, this interchange often occurring many times within a relationship. Who can tell the difference between any ultimate set of opposites?

I venture to assume that not one person reading these words has escaped the telling of lies during this lifetime. If you have told lies then you must understand that others are also at that point of evolution which sees them leaning towards the fabricating of truth too. So be it. Even if you are a truth-teller, or, you sit above that half way point between truth and lies, it must be stated that no such thing exists as absolute anything and certainly not truth!

We are human and must do our best ... **do *your* best** ... that is the operative phrase for every aspect of personal development ... for that is all we can do in search of excellence. It is when we do not do our best that we must question ourselves. Note here that I am emphasising the possessive pronoun, for it is *your* best and not someone else's best that you should be doing. Many people with whom your life contacts will offer opinions, judgements and generally their ideas of just what you should be doing, thinking and saying. Only you know your best. Only you know your aspirations. Only you know your qualities. Only you know your truth.

Only you know you!

Innominate was inherently cognisant of all this merely through contemplation and without physically resorting to the telling or thinking of any lies throughout the majority of a lifetime. In fact the only mendacity hitherto contemplated is within the implication of this chapter's title.

We can put that down to art though can't we?

WHEN TO BEGIN THE MAGICAL EQUATION?

An odd aspect of personal development is that it will eventually come your way regardless of current personal application to the study plus application of it, and resultant service of others it naturally entails. *Why bother putting ourselves out then,* is the obvious question, but it seems irresistible for some of us to continuously push back the barriers of anything including, thankfully, human potential.

If personal development was the universal norm in our society, I cannot vouch for the fact that I would be devoted to its dissemination as I am now. I would probably find myself thrusting forth other alternative viewpoints, equally jarring to some then as are certain of my current personal development viewpoints now! This antagonism to the norm would not be the subject of my actions however, but merely a method of operation, for my goal is forever, *improvement of life through right thinking and doing.*

Sounds slightly pompous, but there you have it. You can have the same goal if you like, there is no patent on it. I took the sentiments from a mixture of my studies which in turn came from a blend of many others. My brand of personal development is merely a further fusion of all I have inspired, commingled with the unique spark which is me, as yours is you, and my art is the way I present it to you.

The reason that personal development will come your way regardless of your present application to it, follows the same line of thinking which sees a public transport system continue to function even though on it lurk riders who have not contributed to it through the agreement of tolls. Fare dodgers exist in all walks of life and not taking responsibility for individual departments of humanity is to our way of thinking the macrocosmic example, yet, I feel that if you were willing to examine the heavens and beyond, you would find great cosmic entities wound up in their own abuses of systems beyond present human conception. You would also find, if you are lucky, those great ones who have forever dedicated themselves to the cause of humanity, no matter how hard that is to believe during times of personal suffering. Don't take my word for it though ... if you have a better explanation then keep it ... if you are feeling altruistic then send it to me for my own benefit, because I cannot prove in concrete tabloid type form what I here write ... I merely sense it, and must point out that many mistakes have been made through following the intuitions of others, and that is why I ask you not to follow mine; rather, get one of your own and follow that!

Now, I am not suggesting that fare dodgers will

not get left behind at some point when it is discovered that they haven't paid their dues, nor is my aim here to subliminally scare you as so often happens more overtly in organised religions; you know what I mean ... *do it or be forever cast into hell ... when the day of judgement comes ... be good and you'll go to heaven, carry on like this and God help you.*

YOU AND ME MAKE THREE is based on the premise that it is impossible to progress individually beyond a certain level, without taking the rest of humanity with you. A sub standard analogy for this could be the Americans giving Marshall Aid to the Germans after defeating them in the latter part of the great 1914-1945 war. Why? It is generally accepted in capitalist economics that it is wise to help fellow nations up to a point of being able to trade with them. *No trade no capitalism no power no glory.* Now I described this as a poor analogy because it concerns necessity for the perpetuation of a political system, whereas the system with which I here deal, is that of evolution, to which politics is but an infinitesimally small part, important nevertheless.

Imagine yourself in that cliché of being cast adrift from civilisation to a desert island, your only company being that of an imbecile. It would be in your interests to educate that person to the point of stimulating conversation and an eventual exchange of viewpoints, *much like trading nations,* before eventually even having that person transcend your teachings into original inspirations of his or her own, *a thought not often enough savoured by teachers!* So it is with personal development, the only way forward for you individually is to spread the word ... this I described perfectly simply in YOU CAN ALWAYS GET WHAT YOU WANT ...

> There is no benefit in keeping this new formula for success to yourself. Knowledge crystallises into a useless obstacle unless you allow it to flow through you into others. You won't steal a better lead on a rival by not telling him or her about your new found wisdom. If you are looking at life with long term vision, then I suggest that the only way forward is to spread the word!

The cynical amongst readers will say that I would write such things, as my sales can only benefit by others disseminating Phil Murray material for me. Yet, it is not really Phil Murray material I wish to spread; what you read in this book is but a morsel of what is on offer once you are willing and able to participate in less oven ready works, to use a metaphor.

So, the time to begin this magical equation of 1+1 equalling 3 knowingly, is now, although you will have unwittingly participated in it since the beginning of your life. Personal development is merely becoming acquainted with inherent capacities, and not as so often interpreted, becoming something you are not. With increasing amounts of inner world exploration, you will get accustomed with yourself, *apart* from what the socialisation process has inculcated into you. This is indeed the problem with mainstream personal development. It vibrates to the sound of the media. Whatever appears in the tabloids, mass viewing television programmes and well attended cinematic offerings, is exactly what the mainstream teachers and lecturers appeal to in human nature ... *if you want to be slim, they'll teach you ... if you want to be a great skier, they'll show you how ... if you want to sell more products, they'll help you ... if you want to be something you are not, they'll tell you that such aspiration is good and stimulating.*

What I am urging is for you to discover yourself.

It doesn't matter if you are not the way the media

says you should be, or different to the general norm within your sphere of operation, it only matters that you increasingly become more yourself! The equation becomes truly magical when two people who are intensifying the essence which can be likened to being themselves, get together in the spirit of interdependent endeavour ... watch out because they'll blow your socks off!

Fashions, trends and phases are personality based and transient, as are quick fix lectures which promise you a world of progress, but which you have forgotten inside the month in which they occurred. The trick you must learn, is to distinguish between your personality oriented desires and your soul purpose. Easy to write about but much harder to accomplish with efficacy. Meditation is the only tool I know of that can help you achieve this, along with study and service of others.

There is no quick fix ... you have to get down to the business of doing it, and this entails time and patience!

Anyone telling you anything other than what you have just read is either after a fast buck, putting you under a spell, or is just plain misinformed. The moment you decide to find out who and what you really are, the magic has begun. The vacillations, ups and downs, the moments of doubt, are all outrageous to a point at which many jump off the boat before it gathers too much momentum; but the wise and tolerant persist and ultimately will be rewarded in ways impossible for the personality to comprehend. As always in this brand of personal development, it is a process of gradual graduation.

And so my friend, let the magic begin, may your journey be a happy one of joy for others in addition to yourself ... your benefit is mine, and with added impetus from those who know, the murderers, rapists, paedophiles, molesters, tricksters, fraudsters, terrorists and fare dodgers, will all benefit too, for without them it is impossible for us all to go forward together.

That is what I mean by YOU AND ME MAKE THREE!

The End

Well, was it good for you? Did the earth move? Will the advanced viewpoints on a latent aspect of human potential help you in your endeavour for self improvement? Has the most explosive equation in history found favour in your heart? Is Innominate real to you?

Most importantly, will you get down to the business of doing it ... you know, really self improving with honest personal development, for that is what this whole business is about; if you merely read the material without instigating positive change into your world, then that is but one statistic ... a book sale for me. If you practically seize the opportunity to evolve with an initiation onto a higher plane of livingness, then you and I can both be happy with our efforts.

We live in an odd world of paradoxes so often daunting when too many obstacles have presented themselves to us in too short a time. The only real obstacle to any accomplishment is however yourself. The power that I so often write about, innate within each human entity, is mostly used by us antagonistically against ourselves. My urge is that we should seize this power for our own and universal good. Energy does not rest, and if you are not manipulating it in some way, shape or form, to suit yourself and the good of humankind, then it surely will find an outlet for itself, and in the main it seems, unguided energy is mischievous.

So, don't just read it ... do it!

1+1=3 and by now you should know it. YOU AND ME MAKE THREE, so don't ever settle for less! Improve compoundly, and remember that nothing stays the same ... it either gets better or worsens. How do you wish your life to progress?

I send you my best wishes for a bright life of peace and tranquillity. I hope that you achieve all that is necessary for the particular process of living in which you find yourself. Be wise, charitable and caring; this way the whole world wins. It is with an understanding of the big picture, *the whole* which is you, me and the rest of humanity, that we can all take one giant step forward, together, each in our own way. This is real personal development ... the type that defines *personal* as referring to THE HUMAN FAMILY.

Love

Phil Murray

FEELING GOOD ABOUT YOURSELF HAS A POSITIVE IMPACT ON EVERYONE AND EVERYTHING AROUND YOU

THE POSITIVE ATTITUDE CLUB

Madeira, Hunts Road, St Lawrence, Isle of Wight PO38 1XT

IF YOU WOULD LIKE TO JOIN WITH US

WELCOME TO THE CONSTANTLY EVOLVING PAC CONCEPT

The Positive Attitude Club accepts applications from anyone able to contemplate beyond the obvious. All we ask is that they embrace the philosophy that positive attitudes are helpful. This is a member's organisation; direction, activities and content ideas are always welcome. In line with our plans for the expansion of this beautifully simple philosophy, every member is invited to begin their own local PAC along the lines of *forward thinking through creative discussion.* In harmony with my own Mission Statement, I shall be available for as many activities as are practical to my own schedule. Large or small, old or young . . . all becomes irrelevant when immersed in inspirational interdependence!

Name ....

Address...

.... Post Code........................

Telephone .... Date of Birth........................

Occupation .... Contribution ....
towards newsletter, and administration

Membership Number........*to be all allocated* ....

LET'S ENJOY TODAY WHILST LOOKING FORWARD TO A ROSY FUTURE

Naturally, I hope you join with us. I also feel it important to point out my experience that many people join expecting something which it seems the PAC does not always deliver. I therefore here affirm that the PAC is only what *you* make of it; how can it be any other way unless Phil Murray turns it into some kind of personality oriented group encouraged into existence for his benefit only. You can make a difference, but not just by following *what is* already.

We look forward to being influenced by you!
Phil Murray
Leader of the PAC

PAC is an acronym for Positive Attitude Club.
The PAC philosophy states simply that improvement of pesonal life through positive attitudes benefits humanity as a whole.
We are an independent non profit making organisation dedicated to peaceful interdependence through creative discussion and forward thinking for the world.